D0811266

RUGBY
WORLD CUP
2007

The Official Book

RUGBY WORLD CUP 2007
The Official Book

Published under licence from the IRB and SNC L'Équipe
by Carlton Books Limited, 20 Mortimer Street, London W1T 3JW

First published in 2007

Design copyright © Prolongations, 2007
Text translation copyright © Carlton Books, 2007

All rights reserved. No part of this publication may be repro-
duced, stored in a retrieval system, or transmitted in any form
or by any means, electronic, mechanical, photocopying,
recording or otherwise, without the prior permission of the
copyright owner and the publishers.

A CIP catalogue record for this book is available from the
British Library

ISBN 978-1-84732-082-7

Text: Nicolas Thomas
Design: Frédéric Loussert
Project editor: Martin Corteel
Project art editor: Paul Chattaway
Production: Lisa French

Printed in Italy

PAGES 6–7.
*Sébastien Chabal on the charge in the pool
match against Namibia.*

PAGES 156–157.
*South African president Thabo Mbeki joins in
the victory celebrations.*

PAGES 158–159.
*A jubilant Bryan Habana dives over for one of
his eight tries.*

RUGBY
WORLD CUP
2007

The Official Book

CARLTON

iRB

RUGBY
WORLD CUP
2007
FRANCE

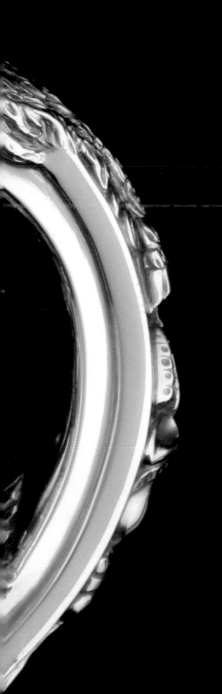

CONTENTS

The Rugby World Cup 2007 will ultimately be remembered as the most successful in the tournament's illustrious 20-year history.

The tremendous festival atmosphere generated across all of the twelve competition venues set the tone for what was to be a spectacular affair as the 20 participating teams delivered what was the most competitive tournament to date.

Few will forget the competitiveness of the so-called smaller Unions; Fiji, Georgia, Namibia, Samoa, Tonga, USA and indeed tournament debutants Portugal all captured the imagination, highlighting the advances that have been made in the past four years with the help of the IRB's unprecedented US$50 million strategic initiatives.

We value our traditions and history in Rugby that are based on fair play, loyalty and friendship. Such characteristics came to the fore during the tournament and I would like to thank the people of France for their tremendous support of the tournament. They volunteered by the thousands and turned up in their millions at the stadiums.

In addition a global audience of over 4 billion watched the drama unfold through their television sets. Indeed the France versus England semi-final attracted a record audience of over 20 million, a first for Rugby, and a figure that rivals that of the Soccer World Cup final held in Paris in 1998. Such strong figures underline the ever advancing growth and popularity of Rugby on a worldwide scale.

Finally, I could not complete this piece without mentioning the tremendous contribution made by those who worked tirelessly to deliver the tournament. The France 2007 Organizing Committee were exceptional in their delivery of key programmes and I would also personally like to thank them for all of their hard work over the past four years and ensuring that the Rugby World Cup 2007 was the huge success expected.

DR SYD MILLAR

CHAIRMAN
RUGBY WORLD CUP LIMITED (RWCL)

The Australian playmaker George Gregan keeps tight control of his pack, but a mistake against England would bring his team's hitherto masterly campaign to an abrupt end in the quarter-finals.

Photo gallery

11

LEFT.
Whether on a Gaelic football jersey or on a Irish four-province flag, green stands for hope in rugby too.

RIGHT.
When Jonny Wilkinson is missing, Jason Robinson takes his place as England's inspirational figure. Robinson was seriously injured in the first round but went on to enjoy a comeback that was as spectacular as that of his team.

The 'Flying Fijians' were finally grounded in the quarter-finals. The admirable Pacific warriors gather their thoughts after giving the future world champions a fright.

Sébastien Chabal's ferocious demeanour gives way to a mask of pain after the cruel defeat of the semi-final.

Rimas Alvarez-Kairelis (right) confronts Simon Easterby, Neil Best and Paul O'Connell (left to right): the Pumas pull the Irish clover apart with a shower of Garryowens.

the
champions

South Africa   Rugby World Champions 2007

The 'Rainbow Nation' on top of the world

The Springboks – powerful, talented and constant – realized their dream by capturing a second world title, twelve years after the first. An immense source of happiness for all South Africans, of all races, while they wait to see a national team that will reflect more closely the people that it represents.

LEFT.
Could the Springboks' fireworks of 2007 rival the exuberance of the 1995 victory on home ground? The team was certainly unable to contain its delight at this 'second child' (in the words of their coach Jake White).

RIGHT.
The South Africans Fourie Du Preez (left) and Bakkies Botha deprive the Englishman Jason Robinson of the ball, before stripping him of his world crown.

JOHN SMIT, clad in a Springbok track-suit, his left eye bearing the marks of the final's physical intensity, was hard put to make his way through the excited crowd as he clutched to his chest the Webb Ellis Cup, now engraved for a second time with the two words 'South Africa'. 'We've worked all our lives to win this cup,' declared the South African captain, 'but it will take us a lifetime to take it in!' Despite their early-morning arrival (6.45 a.m.), the 'Glory Boys' (as they were dubbed the day after the match by the local *Sunday Times*) were greeted by over 5,000 people at the airport in Johannesburg.

A clean sweep of all the honours

The Springboks' baggage contained not only their sport's most coveted trophy but also the titles of 'team of the year', 'player of the year' and the tournament's leading try scorer for Bryan Habana (eight tries, equalling Jonah Lomu's record), 'best coach of the year' for Jake White and leading overall scorer for Percy Montgomery (105 points). And the delegation also included half a dozen indisputable members of an international 'dream team' chosen from the Rugby World Cup 2007: apart from Montgomery at full-back and Habana on

the left wing, places would surely go to Fourie Du Preez at scrum-half, the Juan Smith–Schalk Burger tandem of flankers, and the impeccable lock Victor Matfield, the uncontested king of France's air space throughout the tournament! These outstanding players go a long way to explaining the Springboks' dominance over the sixth Rugby World Cup.

In the extraordinary crush of the main hall in the O.R. Tambo airport in Johannesburg, the magic of 1995 had visibly returned, just as it had done in the previous 48 hours in the streets of Soweto, Cape Town and Durban. For a few days, the 'Rainbow Nation' could forget its financial problems, the ravages of AIDS and the slower than expected

transformation of post-apartheid society – twelve years after the Springboks led by François Pienaar had won the world title at home, on 24 June 1995, in the Ellis Park Stadium in Johannesburg, under the eyes of Nelson Mandela, the first democratically elected president of the Republic of South Africa.

Mandela expresses his confidence

At the age of 89, the 1993 Nobel Prize winner was not strong enough to go to Paris for the final, but his successor and former vice-president Thabo Mbeki was in the Stade de France to share the

BELOW
'We've worked all our lives to win this trophy', declared John Smit, who played the role of captain to perfection throughout the French campaign. 'But it will take us a lifetime to take it in!'

happiness of the Springboks under the golden confetti, watched by television viewers all over the world. Madiba, as Mandela is affectionately known by South Africans, had sent a video message to the players, expressing his confidence in them and evoking the memory of 1995: 'We were, above all, one single nation united behind our victorious team.' Mandela had passed through Paris in September, however, when he had been given a green-and-yellow shirt by John Smit, embellished with his No.2 – just as François Pienaar had done in 1995 with his No.6 shirt, which the then South African president proudly wore when he went on to the pitch in Johannesburg to present the Webb Ellis Cup to the Springbok captain.

The challenge of 'Africanization'

In response to questions from South African journalists about the paucity of non-white players in the winning team, Bryan Habana – one of the two mixed-race members of the side, along with Jon-Paul Pietersen – attempted to defuse the debate by declaring that he wanted 'simply to represent the South African nation': 'Sport is a factor of equality and we are a squad of 47 South Africans proud to be back in our country!'

Jake White was not surprised. He knew that politics would rear its head almost as soon as their feet were on home soil once again. The coach had

anticipated the criticisms by stating that it was important 'not to repeat the mistakes made after the first world title, which was not followed by a transformation of the team' (meaning, an 'Africanization' of the national team of a country with a population that is 75 per cent black and 9 per cent of mixed-race).

It is obvious, in the light of the core 15 chosen by White for the final sprint of the Rugby World Cup 2007, that the advances made in the last twelve years have not been very spectacular: one mixed-race wing in 1995 (Chester Williams), two mixed-race wings in 2007 (Habana and Pietersen). Some members of the ANC, the governing party, have coined the term 'black wing syndrome', to suggest that players like Habana, Pietersen and Ashwin Willemse are little more than smokescreens to obscure the absence of real change.

White: 'It's like having a second child'

'This victory is like giving birth to a second child,' exclaimed the South African coach. 'It's a new opportunity and we must take advantage of it!' Radical commentators have already proposed the application of a '2008 plan' that would involve the appointment of a black coach and the change of the emblem – and therefore the name of the team – from the springbok (a relic of the apartheid regime) to the Kalahari antelope, as well as the introduction of a minimum quota of ten black or mixed-race players in the national team by 2011.

White, in gentlemanly fashion, was keen to deflect the attention away from himself: 'All this goes beyond South African rugby. Just seeing President Mbeki on the shoulders of one of our players with the Webb Ellis Cup, there's no stronger symbol for our country. It's the construction of a nation that is continuing!'

The coach's astute plan

In this somewhat uneasy situation, Percy Montgomery was quick to come

RIGHT.
After the final whistle, all the Springbok players and technical staff embraced each other for an intense prayer, in unison with their people waiting for them thousands of miles away.

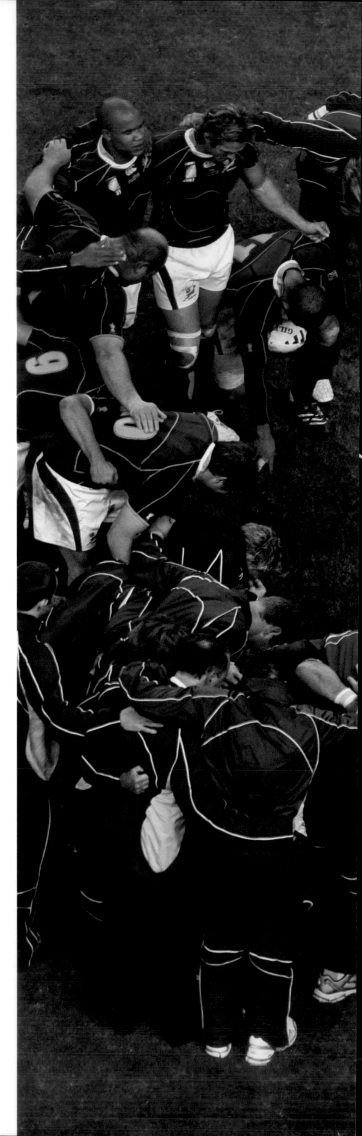

The wheel has turned. As the new champions celebrate, Jonny Wilkinson, the hero of England's triumph in 2003, experiences the desolation of a usurped king.

to the defence of his coach: 'Jake, like the team, has suffered a lot in these last four years, but we are happy to be able to come back to South Africa with the cup. Jake has overcome all that to create a balance between youth and experience. He's managed to achieve cohesion in the team …'

Not the least of White's virtues has indeed been the protection that he has provided his squad from political tensions, along with the astonishing self-confidence that he instilled in them.

Despite the contretemps of the 2006 season (seven defeats in twelve test matches), he calmly stuck to his plan. Above all, he gave little importance to the 2007 Tri Nations, sending a B team to contest the matches in Australia and New Zealand. His sights were set further ahead, on the Stade de France on 20 October 2007!

Since his appointment in 2004 – an unusually long tenure for this post – the Springbok coach has patiently built up a team that blends

young talents (whom he had taken to the under-21 world title in 2002) and hardened players, most notably the recalled prop Os Du Randt, a member of the 1995 world championship team, and the misunderstood pretty boy, Percy Montgomery. Brushing aside criticism, White even recruited Eddie Jones, the Australian coach of the losing Wallaby finalists in 2003, to add sparkle to the three-quarters – without sacrificing the power play that has traditionally

against Tonga. After 47 minutes, the Springboks were clinging on to a narrow lead (10–7)! The entrance of some of the big guns (Smit, Matfield, B.J. Botha, Steyn and Habana) allowed the team to save face, but the close score at the final whistle (30–25) provided food for thought.

A second warning, again with no losses involved, came in the quarter-final against Fiji. Seeing that his teammates had been unsettled after conceding two tries in two minutes (20–20 in the 68th minute), John Smit gathered them together to hammer home the message that they could not lose this match and throw away so many years of sacrifice. The 'White Spirit' made an impression yet again: 37–20 in favour of South Africa at the final whistle.

The only 'Southerners' to emerge unscathed

Luck would have it that the Springboks saw their most daunting obstacles removed from their path over the course of the competition. Argentina's victory in the opening match took the French out of their half of the draw, while their two rivals from the Southern hemisphere, the All Blacks and the Wallabies, made premature exits from the tournament in the quarter-finals – eliminated, respectively, by France and a resuscitated English side.

First Argentina and then England failed to summon the resources needed to stand in the way of Jake White's 'winners' as they heaved themselves to the top of the world. The Webb Ellis Cup returned to Johannesburg, twelve years on, and the 'Rainbow Nation' could continue its reconstruction … ■

In order to beef up his scrum, Jake White brought Os Du Randt (right) out of international retirement. After coming out on top of the English prop Phil Vickery (left), the 35-year-old Springbok, a winner in 1995, joined the highly select club of double world champions.

been a quintessential feature of South African rugby.

The historic triumph of South African clubs in the latest Super 14 can only have instilled more confidence in the Springboks just three months before their departure to France. The first 100 per cent South African final, between the Natal Sharks and the Pretoria Bulls (which became the country's first side to win the trophy) provided a good omen.

Tonga and Fiji, warnings with no losses involved

'I believe in our chances,' repeated Jake White to all and sundry when he posed with his 'bunch of winners' after landing on French soil in a plane named, prophetically, *Hope and Glory*. In their main clash in pool A, the Springboks decimated an English side deprived of their guide, Jonny Wilkinson (36–0). The only false note in the first round was White's sin of pride in resting eleven first-choice players for the match

The beautiful life of Bryan

The South African wing, responsible for eight tries (equalling Jonah Lomu's record for the Rugby World Cup), illuminated the tournament with his talent and played a crucial role in the Springboks' triumph.

Jake White, who had given Bryan Habana his first chance with the Springboks in November 2004, had reason to be proud of his protégé, now a superstar ... and a world champion.

TO ASSESS the popularity of Bryan Habana from Pretoria to Cape Town, it is sufficient to know that, even before his exploits in the Rugby World Cup 2007 and his title of 'best player of 2007', he was known as 'Little Madiba' (Madiba being the nickname given by the 'rainbow' people to its guide, Nelson Mandela himself).

Bearing the first name (Bryan with a 'y') of the former Manchester United footballer Bryan Robson, Habana, the mixed-race kid from Johannesburg, met with mixed success before delighting the staunch traditionalists of the Pretoria Bulls' Loftus Versfeld stadium in Pretoria. The Springbok's 'Mister Perfect' sometimes seems almost too good to be true… When the Natal Sharks were leading 19–13 just seconds from the end of the 2007 Super 14 final, he unleashed a 'Habanesque' recital to score, with a characteristic angelic leap, the try that would make the Bulls the first South African team to win the competition. Habana immediately dedicated this try to his coach, Heineke Meyer,

'to thank him for his support'. How typical of Bryan! Furthermore, his favourite film is Rob Reiner's *A Few Good Men*, he ceaselessly extols 'Christian family values', prefers his name to 'express union rather than an ethnic group' and declares that his favourite food is his mother's home cooking!

In the 75th minute of the semi-final against Argentina, the South African winger sets off, smiling, on an 85-yard sprint that culminated in his eighth try of the tournament.

Under the protection of his father

Humble, respectful, with a permanent smile on his face (his happiness seemed particularly contagious on the podium in the Stade de France, on the night of the final), the Springbok wing is closely protected by his father, Bernie Habana, who has combined his flourishing building materials firm with the management of his son's career since 2003 – one year before Jake White had the bright idea of calling Bryan to the position of centre for his first cap (and first try), against England (16–32) in November 2004. At that time, Bryan had thought that the places in the South Africans' backs were closed to him. After an approach from the ACT Brumbies of Canberra, he had seriously considered the Australian offer, with a view to ultimately earning a place with the Wallabies for the Rugby World Cup in France.

The revelation of 1995

In the highly select King Edward VII School in Johannesburg, cricket and football were the main sports, but Bryan Habana's world was turned upside down by the Rugby World Cup 1995. Accompanied by his father, young Bryan, at the tender age of twelve, attended the opening South Africa–Australia match (27–18) and, above all, the South Africa–New Zealand final (15–12 after extra time) on 24 June 1995. In the stands of the Ellis Park Stadium in Johannesburg, he had a revelation: 'When Joel Stransky's drop goal went through the posts, at 12–12 in extra time, I felt something very strong! At that moment, I had just one dream: to wear the green-and-gold shirt myself one day.'

The next year, in secondary school, Bryan made his rugby debut as a scrum-half and soon made a name for himself through his natural speed, bestowed on him by 'the Man up there', the God who had watched over him with such loving care – to the extent of making him the best player in this, the sixth Rugby World Cup tournament, largely on account of eight tries scored in bursts: four against Samoa (59–7) and two against the United States (64–15) in the pool stage, then a further brace against Argentina (37–13) in the semi-finals.

The aim: to overtake Lomu in 2011

At the moment, Bryan Habana and Jonah Lomu stand shoulder to shoulder in the pantheon of world rugby. They share the same record (eight tries in a single Rugby World Cup) and the same position on the left wing, but that is almost all they have in common. Whereas Habana is a mixed-race kid from an upmarket neighbourhood in Johannesburg, Lomu is the child of Tongan immigrants who grew up in the tough area of Mangere, on the outskirts of Auckland. Their style of play is also worlds apart: whereas 'Speedy' Habana (5 ft 10 in, 14 stone 11 lb) pounces on errors to slip through two opponents like greased lightning, the tank Lomu (6 ft 5 in, 18 stone 8 lb), just as fast at his peak, preferred to crash into defences and smash them to pieces. And, above all, Habana is now a world champion, whereas Lomu will always be a king without a crown.

The young Springbok needs to continue to stay away from enemy tacklers to keep his bones intact and be able, in 2011, to cross the Indian Ocean to dazzle in the 'land of the Big White Cloud'. In the Rugby World Cup in New Zealand he will need to score at least eight more tries to surpass Lomu (and his total of 15 tries in the final phase of the tournament) and become, at the age of 28, the greatest scorer of tries in the history of the competition – thus writing a further chapter that would surely gratify Bryan and his two protectors, the Man up there (God) and the Man down here (his father, Bernie). ∎

Bryan Habana had dreamed of wearing the green-and-gold shirt ever since the Springboks' triumph in 1995. Twelve years later, he holds aloft the Webb Ellis Cup.

30

PLAYER OF THE TOURNAMENT
Bryan Habana

LEFT.
Everybody loves Bryan Habana – young and old, black and white. The mixed-race winger is undoubtedly the most popular rugby player in South Africa.

BELOW.
The rocket man's patented flourish: an angelic leap into his opponents' in-goal area. Habana dives, and his rivals sink.

Twenty teams.
One cup.

A summary of six weeks of competition

1st ROUND

4 pools. 40 matches

POOL A

1. SOUTH AFRICA (19 pts)
2. ENGLAND (14 pts)

3. Tonga (9 pts)
4. Samoa (5 pts)
5. United States (1 pt)

ENGLAND – UNITED STATES: **28–10**

SOUTH AFRICA – SAMOA: **59–7**

TONGA – UNITED STATES: **25–15**

SOUTH AFRICA – ENGLAND: **36–0**

TONGA – SAMOA: **19–15**

SOUTH AFRICA – TONGA: **30–25**

ENGLAND – SAMOA: **44–22**

SAMOA – UNITED STATES: **25–21**

ENGLAND – TONGA: **36–20**

SOUTH AFRICA – UNITED STATES: **64–15**

WAS THE PARC DES PRINCES going to provide the stage, on Friday 28 September 2007, for an unprecedented event in the history of the Rugby World Cup: the shameful downfall of the reigning world champions, eliminated in the first round of the competition? It was true that, six days earlier, the return of 'Wilko the Magnificent' (the fly-half Jonny Wilkinson) had allowed Brian Ashton's players to recover a little of their previous prestige by disposing of Samoa (44–22) but, that same afternoon, the unpredictable Tongans had succumbed to the Springboks by a

PREVIOUS PAGE.
The Tongan Sukanaivalu Hufanga shakes off his pursuers Ollie Barkley (tackling), Andy Gomarsall (No.9) and Matthew Tait to score a try. England's woes were not yet over.

OPPOSITE LEFT.
Lewis Moody (left) and the English had to summon up all their energy to resist the attacks of Pierre Hola and his Tongan colleagues.

England come back from the brink

Behind an imperious South Africa, the reigning world champions avoid the humiliation of a first-round elimination by sidelining a thrilling team from Tonga.

mere five points (25–30) after an exciting match.

As incredible as it may have seemed just a few weeks earlier, the odds were evenly divided for an England–Tonga match that no longer seemed an unequal contest. On one side were the seven islands of Tonga with their 10,000 federated players; on the other, mighty England, the world title-holder with one and a half million players ... The 'Sea Eagles' had had to endure a knock-out decider (against South Korea, 83–3) to book their place for France, having been beaten four times over by Fiji and Samoa in the Oceania zone.

The hungry 'Sea Eagles'

When Nili Latu, the flanker and captain, stepped on to the Paris pitch at the head of his islanders, who still

remembered that terrible 101–10 defeat inflicted on the Tongans by the English in the first round of the Rugby World Cup 1999? Certainly not the English players, who had come to believe – with some justification – that they could well be going back to London the following day. It is difficult to forget the stirring spectacle of the Tonga players performing their traditional dance, the *Sipi Tau*, first a few yards then merely inches away from the 22 players in their red tops, ranked shoulder to shoulder and refusing to bat an eyelid. The men from the Pacific shouted in the faces of their opponents that the 'sea eagle was hungry', that they would show 'no pity' in 'crushing courageous hearts'. All this to the sound of a stirring 'Swing Low, Sweet Chariot', sung with as much anguish as hopefulness by the

Wilkinson and his team-mates stare down their opponents during the Tongan Sipi Tau.

With four tries in the first round, Paul Sackey (here seen scoring against Tonga) was one of the most successful English players.

thousands of English supporters. The combative tone had been set and the very first charge by the No.8 from the Toulouse club, Finau Maka, sent tremors of delight through the the Parc des Princes, which was largely behind the Tongans. Who could have guessed, seeing him sweep his team-mates along in the wake of his imposing hairdo, that this was only his fourth international match?

Wilkinson, tough luck and genius

The players from the Pacific, undoubtedly still feeling the effects of their remarkable resistance against South Africa, held out for only 20 minutes. Long enough, however, to undermine England's confidence still further with a try by Hufanga, the centre from the Brive club, sent through the opposing defence by Taione. But the course of the match was changed in the 19th minute by a flash of brilliance ... from Jonny Wilkinson. Instead of converting a penalty, he dreamed up a miraculous kick, perfectly weighted on a diagonal to Paul Sackey, who was unmarked on the right wing. Pure genius had struck, requiring only Sackey's speed and agility to finish off an unforgettable try. The triumphant 85-yard sprint by the powerful Wasps winger in the 38th minute made him the man of the match and sealed the match for England. The last minutes of the match enabled the Tongans, swept along by the French crowd, to score a second try from a lunge down the left wing by the flanker Pole. At 36–20, the score was now fairer and Kutusi Fielea's men could kneel in a circle, their index fingers pointing at the Parisian sky for one final prayer, before proudly bowing

ABOVE.
England received a heavy blow when the excellent Jason Robinson was injured against South Africa.

out of this Rugby World Cup 2007.

Two days later, the Springboks also completed their task by dominating the American Eagles 64–15. Having landed at Roissy airport aboard a plane christened *Hope and Glory*, they barely had to exert themselves in pool A to follow the path laid out by their coach, Jake White: a simple straight line pointing inexorably to a final victory on 20 October in the Stade de France, 'and nothing less'!

Vickery: 'A funereal atmosphere'

The first weekend of the tournament had given some indications about the situation of the forces competing in pool A. Jonny Wilkinson had not escaped from his run of bad luck and the English would have to manage without their charismatic fly-half. He had been injured 12 times in the previous four

years and had participated in only eight Tests since his consecration in Sydney. This time, an ankle twisted in a routine training session banished the strategist from Newcastle to the stands, leaving his team-mates prey to the doubts that had pursued them since the Rugby World Cup. The English team's play on 8 September was indeed hesitant against the 'Eagles' in the Bollaert stadium in Lens and they beat the United States by merely 28–10 – the narrowest margin ever against the Americans. England scored only three tries and so failed to earn an offensive bonus. The 106–8 thrashing in August 1999 seemed to belong to the distant past as the uninspired English displayed severe deficiencies in their attacking game. After confessing that 'the atmosphere back in the dressing room was like a funeral', Phil Vickery nevertheless considered that his

comrades were capable of raising their game before Friday 14 September in response to the challenge posed by South Africa in the Stade de France – an encounter that 'Raging Bull' Vickery himself would miss, following a two-match suspension for tripping up the American centre Paul Emerick.

The next day in the Parc des Princes, John Smit's South Africa dampened the ardour of the Samoans (59–7), although the latter, encouraged by the Parisian spectators with cries of 'Allez les Bleus', gave way only in the 33rd minute, after a run by the uncatchable winger from Pretoria, Bryan Habana. He scored the first of his four tries by darting through the Samoan defence like a SuperBall catapulted at full pelt along the walls of a corridor.

BELOW LEFT.
Even the redoubtable English pack had to bow before the power of the Springboks.

BELOW RIGHT.
Mahonri Schwalger's Samoans (left, facing the South African Os Du Randt) had hoped to create a surprise, but they had to leave the role of upstart to their Tongan neighbours.

Confronted by the Samoan David Lemi, the Springbok Percy Montgomery scores five of the 29 points he clocked up that day.

The Springboks give a demonstration

The South Africa–England match on Friday 14 September in the Stade de France promised to provide pool A with a stirring climax. The English world champions, still deprived of Wilkinson, had to confront the Springboks at their most dangerous – four years after the same confrontation in the pool stage in Perth, which had finished 25–6 in favour of a supremely confident English team.

Having deliberately allowed his players to cruise through the 2007 Tri Nations and finish last, in order to protect them, Jake White, the South African coach, did not skimp on praise for his squad, insisting that it had 'reached maturity'. It consisted largely of players with whom he had won the crown of under–21 world champions in 2002, although young talents like the winger Bryan Habana (aged 24), the flanker Schalk Burger (24) and the gifted Natal Sharks fly-half François Steyn (just turned 20) were shrewdly combined with battle-hardened warriors like John Smit and Victor Matfield.

It was a thoroughly dejected England that prostrated themselves 0–36 that afternoon, the apparent victims of an unfathomable curse: with their two star fly-halves sidelined through injury, the team now suffered the loss of Jason Robinson. The 33-year-old Sale full-back, one of the few to hold his head above the tide, pulled his left hamstring in the 56th minute … The English, seemingly doomed to chasing the ball without ever catching it, conceded the first try in the sixth minute, at the hands of Juan Smith. The Springboks' realism and speed of execution never allowed the world champions to recover from this blow. The omens did not seem promising for Ashton's men in their forthcoming encounters with first Samoa and then Tonga.

Tonga gives South Africa a shock

Jake White, in contrast, had few worries about the match against Tonga on Saturday 22 September in the Bollaert stadium in Lens, and even opted to rest 11 of his star players. Signs of over-confidence, perhaps: the 'Sea Eagles' had come out unconvincing winners

against the United States (25–15) and then Samoa (19–15), but they were not content with being mere 'grains of sand' in world rugby (in the words of their lock Inoke Afeaki) and were intent on a place in the quarter-finals. In the face of an onslaught from the islanders, White had to take emergency action in the 47th minute, shortly after a charging try from the right prop Kisi Pulu gave Tonga a 10–7 lead. In one fell swoop, White brought on Matfield, Smit, Steyn, Habana and B.J. Botha to avoid one of the biggest surprises in the history of the Rugby World Cup. Three South African tries in six minutes should have been sufficient to quell the revolt (27–10 in favour of the Springboks, 65th minute) but the Tongans would have further moments of glory: between minutes 70 and 77, they scored two tries (from Hufanga, following a kick by Hola, and Vaki, after a counter-attack from the Tongan 22-metre line), and they finished off a mere five points adrift of the

South Africans, to the acclaim of the 40,000-strong crowd in Lens.

A few minutes later, the English, with Wilkinson at No.10, faced up to Samoa in the Beaujoire stadium in Nantes. Asserting themselves by 44–22 (including 24 points from their master strategist), England gained some consolation … Their match against Tonga was squaring up, more than ever, as a veritable sudden-death battle – and a possible source of enormous humiliation.

A world away from the stress of England's last-minute escape, the final match in this round was a formality for the South Africans, who dominated Peter Thorburn's Americans in Montpellier by 64–15. On this occasion, the Eagles' young left wing Thretton Palamo became, at the age of 19 years and eight days, the youngest player ever to take part in a Rugby World Cup. ■

ABOVE.

Henry Bloomfield's Americans, despite offering resistance against England, Tonga and Samoa, had to come to terms with coming last in their pool.

Shaken by the Tongan onslaught (Inoke Afeaki, left), South Africa had to quickly bring on its star substitutes, such as John Smit, in order to avoid a huge upset.

The striking hairstyle and furious charges of Finau Maka made him the attraction of the first round.

Finau Maka
The great blue of the Pacific

Man of the Pool

LOOK NO FURTHER FOR THE SIXTH member of the Jackson Five – he is called Finau and prefers rugby to soul music. With his abundant Afro, which easily adds an extra seven inches to his height of 6ft 3in, Tonga's No.8 was the star of the first round of the Rugby World Cup 2007. Nicknamed 'Jimi Hendrix' and 'The Rock', Finau Maka, the 13th child of a family of 14, waited to his 30th birthday before making his debut with the Tongan team, against the American Eagles (25–15). And he did it in devastating style: the first cap, the first match of the Rugby World Cup, the first try, in the first minute!

The fact was that the younger brother of the former All Black Isitolo Maka had been waiting for a signal from the French coach Bernard Laporte. A member of the Toulouse team since the 2001–02 season, Finau waited and waited but the call never came – despite his dazzling seasons for Toulouse, first on the wing then as No.8, despite his repeated declarations of love to the media ('Wearing the French shirt would be a huge honour for me'). The Tongan Federation had already put out feelers before the Rugby World Cup 2003 in Australia, but Finau had turned down the offer.

When Kutusi Fielea took over the 'Sea Eagles' in April 2007, he managed to convince Finau to trade his dreams of the blue of France for a few weeks of Pacific adventure. And although Finau still stumbles slightly over the words and choreography of the *Sipi Tau* (the Tongan version of the *haka*), he quickly became the natural leader of Tonga's XV: 'He's so powerful', enthused his captain Nili Latu. 'We feel his physical presence and his knowledge of the game at difficult moments.'

Although Maka was the best Tongan player in the decisive match against England, he was unable to prevent the world champions from exerting their superiority on the pitch (20–36). However, when Kutusi Fiela expresses his hopes for the Rugby World Cup 2011, the 30-year-old player from Toulouse reminds him that, after only four matches, he is still a young international!

POOL B

1. AUSTRALIA (20 pts)
2. FIJI (15 pts)

3. Wales (12 pts)
4. Japan (3 pts)
5. Canada (2 pts)

AUSTRALIA – JAPAN: **91–3**

WALES – CANADA: **42–17**

FIJI – JAPAN: **35–31**

AUSTRALIA – WALES: **32–20**

FIJI – CANADA: **29–16**

WALES – JAPAN: **72–18**

AUSTRALIA – FIJI: **55–12**

CANADA – JAPAN: **12–12**

AUSTRALIA – CANADA: **37–6**

FIJI – WALES: **38–34**

IN POOL B, IN WHICH AUSTRALIA had ensured their qualification the weekend before, the decisive Wales–Fiji match on Saturday 29 September, in the Beaujoire stadium in Nantes, was undoubtedly the most gripping and spectacular game in the first round of the Rugby World Cup 2007. Like the England–Tonga match (36–20) of the previous evening, this winner-take-all contest in some respects pitted the old empire against the New World. On this occasion, the audience in Nantes witnessed rugby at its most attractive, with both teams united by a common aim: to cross their opponents' goal line by means of brain or brawn. Before this contest, the statistics hardly favoured the players from the Pacific, who had a record of six defeats in six matches against the Red Devils. When fly-half

The Fijian surprise

While Australia won all their matches in impressive style, the Fijians took Wales's scalp in a magnificent contest to grab a place in the quarter-finals.

Nicky Little was asked about his team's chances, he replied, with an ironic allusion to the Fijians' reputation: 'It all depends whether we're asleep under the coconut trees or whether we all move forward together.'

Rauluni: 'I'm so proud'

What a pity that, while his team-mates were making an interminable lap of honour after their superb qualification (38–34), Nicky Little lay sprawled on a stretcher, the victim of bad luck and a Welsh push in the last minute of play that toppled him backwards with his leg wedged in a loose scrum. The hugs of his jubilant team-mates would change nothing – for Little, the Rugby World Cup was over, whereas for Rabeni,

Qera, Delasau and the rest it had taken on a new, almost unreal dimension for this small country of more than 300 islands and just 825,000 inhabitants. It was the islanders from Fiji who would go to Marseille to face the Springboks in the quarter-finals! Twenty years after their first incursion into this phase of the tournament (a 16–31 defeat against France), the 'Flying Fijians' were again going to experience the unique excitement of being among the world's top eight.

'A few years ago, we would have lost that match,' ruminated Mosese Rauluni, the Fijian captain and scrum-half for the Saracens. 'I'm so proud of the lads.' It had indeed demanded great strength of character from the Fijians to resist when the Welsh, playing with 15 against 14, came back from the doldrums (trailing 3–25 in the 25th minute) to score three tries in six minutes before the break and take the lead in the 51st minute (29–25). Never mind that this revival was partly due to a yellow card

PREVIOUS PAGE.
The little Welsh genius Shane Williams crashes into a wall in the decisive match against Fiji, under the worried gaze of his colleague Colin Charvis (right).

OPPOSITE LEFT.
Vilimoni Delasau, a leading light of the dazzling Fijian three-quarters, could savour the exploits of his team, which qualified for the quarter-finals for the first time in 20 years.

unjustly given to Akapusi Qera, the flanker who plays for Gloucester, but it was impossible to remain unaware of the brilliant rainbow straddling the sky in the 45th minute when the diminutive Welsh wing Shane Williams wove together a series of swerves and dummies before touching down over the Fijian goal line with a grin on his face.

Wales banished into the wilderness

However, the islanders' extraordinary opening burst, rewarded by three tries, and the unquenchable thirst for attack of their three-quarters Bai, Rabeni and Delasau deserved a better fate. The Fijians continued to make the running, even at the risk of a counter-attack, as occurred in the 73rd minute, when the Welsh flanker Martyn Williams intercepted a careless pass from Nicky Little to score his side's fourth try (34–31). Gareth Jenkins's players undoubtedly thought that this would be the knock-out blow, but the Fijians, in the words of their captain, 'searched the depths of their souls' and went back to the attack from the Welsh 22-metre line. The 37,000 spectators rose to their feet to participate in the upset that could suddenly be glimpsed on the horizon: the Fijians approached the goal line in the 78th minute, Delasau was tackled by Martyn Williams two feet from the line, but the left prop Graham Dewes was on hand to pick up the ball and touch it down to earn a place in the next round. The Welsh were left to rue Stephen Jones's two conversions and a

The Rugby World Cup was still an ongoing concern for the Fijians, although not for their fly-half Nicky Little, seriously injured against Wales.

Even when deprived of his comrade-in-arms Stephen Larkham, out with a knee injury, George Gregan expertly steered the Australian team to the quarter-finals.

penalty that had struck the goalposts. As for the Fijians, they had succeeded in compensating for the vulnerability of their scrum through their impressive handling. Their incredible attacking play, virtually unmarred by error, and their unfailing ability to move the ball around at high speed had done the rest, launching them to the Stade-Vélodrome in Marseille for an unexpected quarter-final against the Springboks!

The Australian clean sweep

The Australians, for their part, had calmly completed their pool stage two hours earlier in rainy Bordeaux, by effortlessly inflicting a 37–6 defeat on Canada. The Wallabies thus achieved a clean sweep and scoring the maximum of 20 points – hardly surprising, given

the nature of the opposition offered to George Gregan's team, the last to beat the All Blacks (20–15 in the June 2007 Tri Nations). The right wing Drew Mitchell scored two tries to obtain a total tally of seven, making him the highest scorer in the first round, while John Connolly kept his wonder kid Berrick Barnes under wraps, ready for a prospective quarter-final from which the old warhorse Stephen Larkham was ruled out through injury. The Australians had learned the night before that they would face England on Saturday 6 October in Marseille, offering them a chance to avenge that painful final in 2003 (lost at home 17–20 in extra time). 'That defeat in 2003', explained Stephen Larkham, 'is the reason that prompted some of us to

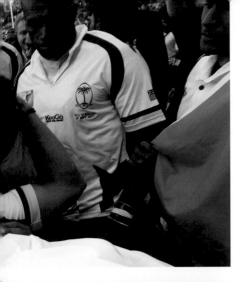

TOP.
The Wallaby Stirling Mortlock (right) catches an up-and-under with aplomb, while the Welshman James Hook falls on his back.

CENTRE.
The Fijians also have to submit to the domination of the Australians, the masters of Pool B.

BELOW.
Shane Williams scores against Japan. Despite the sparkling performances of their wing, the Welsh proved unable to qualify for the next round.

keep going until this Rugby World Cup 2007.' Even the younger players expressed a similar desire for revenge, as in the case of the flanker Rocky Elsom: 'I didn't play, but that still burns me up inside!' Who could be expected to stomach a world title stolen at home in the last minute of extra time by a fateful drop goal? Who would not relish vengeance when the chance to cross swords with the nemesis of Sydney, Jonny Wilkinson, finally presented itself?

The heroic Japanese

The Australian campaign had begun gently on Saturday 8 September in the Gerland stadium in Lyon with an awesome 91–3 victory at the expense of Japan. A tough start for John Kirwan's

Asian side, but then the rugby world can often be very hard on its minnows. Thirteen tries to none, and a mere training session for the Australians.

Four days later, the Fijians made a laboured entrance to the tournament by putting a mere four points between themselves and this same Japanese side (35–31). They spent the last three minutes of the match held back behind their 22-metre line by Japan's 'Cherry Blossoms', who were helped by the 35,000 spectators in the Toulouse stadium to overcome their weariness. Raulini & Co., sloppy in attack and lacking in resources against the attacking zeal of the Japanese, had undoubtedly imagined an easier introduction to the competition ...

The Japanese Hare Makiri (No.6) repels the Canadians Ryan Smith and Dave Spicer. The Asian team would go on to snatch a draw in injury time.

The superiority of the South

On Saturday 15 September, in Cardiff's Millennium Stadium, the Welsh played host to John Connolly's Australians for the second North–South clash of the tournament, after the South Africa–England match (36–20) in the Stade de France the day before. This was a less gruelling match, but the outcome was the same: a marked superiority on the part of the players from the Southern hemisphere, who led 25–3 at half-time. The Welsh managed to make their presence felt in the second half, but without ever challenging the authority of the Australians (final score: 32–20). Above all, this match provided European fans the opportunity to discover the young fly-half from the Queensland Reds, Berrick Barnes. At the age of 21, in only his second international, he was suddenly plunged into the uproar of the Millennium Stadium, on account of Stephen Larkham's right knee, which had unfortunately given out during the previous day's training session. The peroxide kid was not fazed by the occasion and sent Matt Giteau on his way for a try in the 15th minute after an exquisite dummy pass. He paid dearly for this, finding himself face down in the grass for a while after Gareth Thomas roughly crashed into his shoulder. Stirling Mortlock asserted his authority as captain by paying Thomas back in kind a few minutes later with a bruising tackle, giving notice that messing with the new star of Australian rugby would not go unpunished. Eight days later, on Sunday 23

ABOVE.
Drew Mitchell struck three times against Vilimoni Delasau's Fijians. The Australian would be the top scorer in the first round, with seven tries.

OPPOSITE.
Hugh McMeniman breaks through the Canadian defence. The Wallabies passed effortlessly through the pool stage.

September, the Australia–Fiji match in the Mosson stadium in Montpellier would permit a more accurate assessment of the gulf separating Gregan and his cohorts from the other teams in the pool. With a score of 55–12, the Australians dispensed harsh treatment, although John Connolly's displeasure ('We took a while to get going … There were times when, mentally, we were not in the match,') revealed the bitter fate that would have awaited the Fijians if the Wallabies had taken their task more seriously. For one thing, there was no try from the left wing Lote Tuqiri, a native of Sigatoka in Fiji facing his former compatriots on the day of his 28th birthday, but his team-mates scored a total of seven tries, with the wing Drew Mitchell achieving a hat-trick. In order to protect his two metronomes (George Gregan, who had just equalled the record for games played as captain – held by the Englishman Will Carling – and Berrick Barnes), Connolly took them off after an hour of play. This did not prevent the Australians from scoring three new tries, albeit without showing any true conviction. Some of the key players undoubtedly had their minds on the quarter-finals … As for the Fijians, they quickly put this crushing defeat behind them to display their finest attacking rugby against the Welsh, under the autumn sun of the Beaujoire stadium. The challenge was surely a lesser one against a nation from the Northern hemisphere… ■

Berrick Barnes, aged just 21, proved a revelation to Nathan Sharpe (left) and Lote Tuqiri (to the rear), as well as to the spectators. Barnes proved himself a worthy successor to Stephen Larkham.

Man of the Pool

Berrick Barnes
Fearless aplomb

THE PAIN THAT SHOT THROUGH Stephen Larkham's knee during a training session the day before the Wales–Australia clash (20–32) seemed to be a bad omen for the Wallabies. However, the 26 minutes that the young Berrick Barnes (aged 21) spent on the pitch for his international debut against Japan (with two tries to his credit) had confirmed John Connolly's keen instinct. After a low-key season with the Queensland Reds, Barnes was the 30th and last name to join the list for the tournament. When Connolly set off to Europe, he was looking far beyond the Rugby World Cup 2007 and saw Berrick Barnes as the new Larkham of Australian rugby.

The coach had been struck not only by the quality of Barnes' running and kicking but also by his incredible aplomb. The proof came in the 15th minute of the match against Wales, with the dummy pass that set up the try for Matt Giteau and left Barnes on the ground, flattened by a late tackle by Gareth Thomas. It needed more than that, however, to intimidate this lad from Brisbane. His drop goal in the 22nd minute was the perfect response. Eight days later, in the Australia–Fiji game (55–12), Barnes even scored a second drop goal, thereby equalling Stephen Larkham's total in 102 matches …

'Some players reach the top then wonder if they're really in the right place, but Berrick does not have these kind of doubts,' reckons Connolly. 'He is young, but he's already a tough nut!' A tough nut who, as the rookie of the group, was nevertheless entrusted with a mission of the utmost importance: looking after Wally the wallaby, the team's small green and yellow mascot, complete with a red cap. At the same time, the entire Australian squad took great care of its new wonder boy, with Stirling Mortlock protecting him on the pitch. Off it Chris Latham heaped praise on him after his performance against the Welsh: 'Berrick was sensational,' he said. 'His performance perfectly sums up his character and everything he can bring to Australian rugby.'

POOL C

1. NEW ZEALAND (20 pts)
2. SCOTLAND (14 pts)
3. Italy (9 pts)
4. Romania (5 pts)
5. Portugal (1 pt)

NEW ZEALAND – ITALY: **76–14**

SCOTLAND – PORTUGAL: **56–10**

ITALY – ROMANIA: **24–18**

NEW ZEALAND – PORTUGAL: **108–13**

SCOTLAND – ROMANIA: **42–0**

ITALY – PORTUGAL: **31–5**

NEW ZEALAND – SCOTLAND: **40–0**

ROMANIA – PORTUGAL: **14–10**

NEW ZEALAND – ROMANIA: **85–8**

SCOTLAND – ITALY: **18–16**

A huge black shadow

New Zealand confirmed their status as the runaway favourites to win the Cup by crushing the rest of their pool. The Portuguese newcomers won over the hearts of the public, while the Scots scraped through to the quarter-finals.

WHAT IS THERE to say about Pool C except that it spent the three weeks of the first round under the imposing black shadow of 30 players from New Zealand? Their statistics after the last match in the pool, in which they completely overwhelmed Romania 85–8, were instructive: 309 points scored, 35 conceded and, it goes without saying, 20 points out of a possible 20! Only the absence of any real contest (even the 'clash' with Scotland in Edinburgh on 23 September proved a mere formality that ended 40–0) advised caution before jumping to the conclusion that this time the generation of Dan Carter, Richie McCaw and Jerry Collins would not miss its appointment with history. Twenty years after winning the title at home, would the All Blacks finally escape the curse that seemed to prevent the 'best team in the world' capturing the Webb Ellis Cup again?

Oliver: 'The favourite is the team that's going to win …'

In the build-up to the tournament, the experienced hooker Anton Oliver evaded the umpteenth question about the All Blacks' position as runaway favourites: 'The favourite for the championship is the team that's going to win …' This was not enough, however, to divert the spotlight from them. The Kiwis' record since the Rugby World Cup 2003 would instil fear in even the bravest of sides: 38 wins in 43 matches (88 per cent success rate) and an average margin of 20 points in their favour! Not only that: the New Zealanders had not been defeated in 20 matches against countries from the Northern hemisphere. Their five 'failures' occurred against South Africa (three times) and Australia (twice, including that of 30 June 2007 in Melbourne, 15–20, in the Tri Nations cup).

Far from home, but nevertheless carrying the burden of the 'hopes of a nation', the All Blacks went as far as teasingly confessing their trepidation, after the pool stage, at the prospect of unexpectedly facing France in the quarter-finals in Cardiff. In the light of the first phase, however, such remarks seemed mere demonstrations of politeness. Or perhaps the New Zealanders were still mindful of the semi-final they lost at Twickenham on 31 October 1999 (31–43) against the self-same France – a team at that time, moreover, not rated at all either by bookmakers or experts. Byron Kelleher, Reuben Thorne and Anton Oliver, the only survivors of that unimaginable calamity, were still haunted by the half-hour of madness that had allowed Raphaël Ibañez and his men to turn round a match that Jonah Lomu & Co. seemed to have perfectly under control (going from 10–24 down to 43–27 up in 28 minutes!). If the French had prevented an All Black triumph once …

PREVIOUS PAGE.
Dan Carter (No.10), the master technician, congratulates Doug Howlett (No.14), the leading New Zealand scorer in a powerful All Black line-up.

OPPOSITE LEFT.
The All Black flanker Rodney So'oialo sweeps all before him, including the unfortunate Portuguese prop Cristian Spachuck.

RIGHT.
The Romanian team led by Cezar Popescu (left) came away with the consolation prize of a narrow win over Portugal (14–10).

ABOVE.
The Italian prop Martin Castrogiovanni tries his best to stop the All Black scrum-half Byron Kelleher.

Italy overrun by a black tide

The New Zealanders' first outing, on Saturday 8 September in Marseille, was disarmingly easy. However much the Italians huddled round their captain Marco Bortolami to avoid the spectacle of the *haka* and the grimaces of the Kiwi prop Ali Williams, there was no contest on the pitch of the Stade-Vélodrome. Against a Transalpine team that has been consistently rising in the European hierarchy (victories against Wales and Scotland in the 2007 Six Nations Tournament), the All Blacks scored the first of their 11 tries after just 75 seconds of play! The giant Chris Jack grabbed the ball in a lineout, Richie McCaw hurtled forward and the job was done. Five minutes later, Byron Kelleher, amid a thrusting group of Kiwis, provided a pass for another charge by McCaw. The score was already 14–0, but the Kiwi party was only just beginning. 'It is the mark of great teams that they know how to kill the match at the start', acknowledged Pierre Berbizier, the French coach of the 'Nazionale' – and a gracious loser. Doug Howlett's hat-trick enabled him to join Chris Cullen at the head of the list of All Black try scorers, with a total of 46. The only blemish on an otherwise perfect afternoon was the fact that the New Zealand defence let through two tries: one from an interception by the Bristol wing Marco Stanojevic (38th minute), who could not conceal his joy even before touching down, then another from a superb kick by the centre Mirco Bergamasco that he himself followed up (71st minute). The Italians could even have scored a third time in the 77th minute after a confused movement following a chip by fly-half Roland de Marigny, but the try was disallowed by the video referee.

Historic first try for the Portuguese

The next day, in the Geoffroy-Guichard stadium in Saint-Étienne, the Rugby World Cup welcomed its uninhibited young debutants, 'Os Lobos' (the Wolves) from Portugal, the second smallest federation represented in the tournament (4,300 members, as against 1,870 in Georgia). Having emerged victorious against Uruguay in the play-offs (12–5, 12–18), Vasco Uva and his comrades were eager to test themselves

Wearing shirts curiously similar to those of the All Blacks, the Scots had a bad day. Even this break by Simon Webster, opposed by Doug Howlett, failed to open the scoring for them (0–40).

BELOW.
The courage of the Portuguese Luis Pissarra (right) could not prevent the New Zealander Andrew Hore from scoring, but it did earn him the admiration of the public.

against the Scots before confronting their role models, McCaw's All Blacks.

By their own admission, the level of the Portuguese players – several of whom had graduated from sevens – was equivalent to that of the lower reaches of the French Second Division. The best they could hope for was not to let the side down by displaying courage and a 'good dose of pride'. Despite making more than 40 tackles in the first ten minutes, the heroic Portuguese defence finally buckled. Its pack, particularly the left prop Rui Cordeiro, was too overwhelmed to hold firm for long. However, the eight tries conceded against the Scots should not be allowed to completely overshadow the Wolves' first try in the Rugby World Cup: in the 28th minute, a Scottish defensive slip allowed fly-half Pedro Cardoso to pass to the left wing Pedro Carvalho, who slipped but still managed to lunge over the goal line to score this historic try. Another consolation awaited Tomaz Morais's team: the Portuguese captain, the flanker Vasco Uva, was chosen as the 'man of the match'.

Portugal beats New Zealand... at football

The match played on Saturday 15 September in the Gerland stadium in Lyon, under the sun of an Indian summer, was one of extreme contrasts, with the 22nd team in the IRB classification pitted against the world's number one. It gave rise to the highest score in the tournament (108–13) and some of the most stirring images of the Rugby World Cup 2007. In the interests of precision, it should be pointed out that this was not the most decisive walkover in the tournament's history – that honour goes to Australia against Namibia in 2003 (142–0) – but it did not fall far short.

Before the contest, some observers were even concerned about the physical wellbeing of the Portuguese amateurs, particularly the young full-back Pedro Leal (5ft 7in and 11st 7lb). This exasperated the lock Gonçalo Uva ('We consider it a lack of respect'), although, at 6ft 6in and 16st 12lb, he admittedly came out well in any assessment of 'competitive' measurements.

57

RIGHT.
Alessandro Troncon
scores the only try in
the Scotland–Italy
match after Rory
Lamont fumbles an
up-and-under.

At the end of the match, the Portuguese (who had even registered a try, scored by the prop Cordeiro in the 46th minute) earned not only a standing ovation from the 40,000 spectators in the Gerland stadium but also an affectionate guard of honour from the All Blacks. The faces of the Portuguese players revealed their admiration for the New Zealand stars, in acknowledgement of the rugby lesson they had just received. The conviviality of the moment was genuine, and it was followed by a seven-a-side football game between the two teams' substitutes, which the Portuguese won 3–1, and then a few beers shared in the Portuguese changing room. 'An unforgettable day' for the 'Lobos' – and for all rugby fans.

Scotland snatch their ticket to the next round

The Scotland–Italy match disputed on Saturday 29 September just a few miles away, in the Geoffroy-Guichard stadium in Saint-Étienne, was worlds away from this bucolic encounter. It was one of the most closely contested matches in the final stages of the pool stage. Both teams were on a knife edge, straggling far behind the All Blacks (the 40–0 defeat inflicted on Jason White & Co. six days earlier in Edinburgh speaks for itself). Pierre Berbizier's Italians and Frank Hadden's Scots faced a winner-take-all game, with the losers destined to board a plane back home the following day

BELOW.
The Portuguese, led by
the centre Miguel
Portela, salute the
spectators in Toulouse,
who cheered them on
constantly in their fine
match against
Romania (10–14).

and make their exit from the Rugby World Cup...

If they did not want to perish in the den of the Greens (the famous footballers of A.S. Saint-Étienne), the Scottish thistles needed to recover some of their traditional prickliness against the unremitting Italian pack, led by the No.8 Sergio Parisse and skilfully manoeuvred by a man as experienced as he is explosive, Alessandro Troncon. The Italian scrum-half, who plays for the Clermont Auvergne club, even found himself captain once again for a day, in the absence of the lock Marco Bortolami, the side's lineout specialist, excluded due to a cervical injury. In this type of decisive match, where nerves and cunning count as much as leg power, the Italians posed a threat, even

though they had been disappointing throughout the pool stage and had failed to fulfil the hopes inspired by their admirable performance in the 2007 Six Nations Tournament, particularly their triumph at Murrayfield in February (37–17).

The rematch turned out to be tense but unspectacular, illuminated only by six penalties from Chris Paterson on the Scottish side and a brief flash of Troncon's guile when he took advantage of Rory Lamont's fumbling of an Italian up-and-under to mystify the Scottish defence and score the only try of the match (12th minute). The fraught closing minutes saw the Italians, trailing 16–18, trying desperately to overtake their rivals via a drop goal, but to no avail ...

BELOW.
The kicking of Chris Paterson (six penalties) allowed Scotland to erase the disaster in Murrayfield (17–37) in February, against the very same Italians, and go through to the quarter-finals.

The Scots were semi-finalists in 1991 and had not failed to make the tournament's top eight since 1987. The players who had postponed their honeymoon to prepare for the Rugby World Cup 2007 could return to their wives with their heads held high. ■

Man of the Pool

ALTHOUGH HE claimed to be unperturbed, Doug Howlett must have thought that the young Fijians Josevata Rokocoko and Sitiveni Sivivatu had definitively replaced him in the battle plans of New Zealand's strategist, Graham Henry. Absent from the European tour in November 2006 because of a sprained knee, and not even included in the 22-strong list for the 'conditioning window' (physical preparation period), Howlett was now the No.4 choice for the position of wing, having also been passed by Rico Gear of the Canterbury Crusaders. In addition, Adidas had just chosen Gear instead of

Doug Howlett
Back in Black

him to shoot an advertising spot alongside Dan Carter and Richie McCaw – a real slap in the face for handsome Doug, who has always enjoyed gracing the covers of magazines. Howlett had therefore been obliged to concentrate on his Super 14 matches with the Auckland Blues and hope that his record would end up speaking for itself: before the Rugby World Cup 2007, he had already scored 43 tries from 59 matches wearing the black shirt!

In the opinion of some members of the Kiwi squad, his excellent finishing and sprinting – he was New Zealand's junior 100-metre champion with 10.76 seconds, although his best time would be 10.68! – did not entirely make up for his signs of nervousness on big occasions. Howlett, however, had responded to his detractors by improving his kicking skills. Having finally earned his place on the French trip, the future right wing for the Irish province Munster was eager to prove himself. He scored six tries in three matches (three against Italy, two against Scotland and one against Romania), bringing his international tally to 49, beating the Kiwi record of 46, previously held by Chris Cullen. This feat was admittedly achieved in a team sailing on very calm water: with 46 tries in four matches, the All Blacks had done little more than warm up for the decisive test of the last eight!

Although Doug Howlett is no longer the first choice on the wing, he made his place in All Black history by beating Chris Cullen's record total of tries.

POOL D

1. ARGENTINA (18 pts)
2. FRANCE (15 pts)

3. Ireland (9 pts)
4. Georgia (5 pts)
5. Namibia (0 pts)

ARGENTINA – FRANCE: **17–12**

IRELAND – NAMIBIA: **32–17**

ARGENTINA – GEORGIA: **33–3**

IRELAND – GEORGIA: **14–10**

FRANCE – NAMIBIA: **87–10**

FRANCE – IRELAND: **25–3**

ARGENTINA – NAMIBIA: **63–3**

GEORGIA – NAMIBIA: **30–0**

FRANCE – GEORGIA: **64–7**

ARGENTINA – IRELAND: **30–15**

PREVIOUS PAGE.
The Argentinean
Martin Scelzo advan-
ces implacably, eva-
ding the Irishman
Geordan Murphy,
whose star team-mate
Brian O'Driscoll
(No.13) is on the
ground: a perfect
summary of the out-
come of Pool D.

OPPOSITE LEFT.
Rémy Martin, the
unlucky hero of the
opening match, is
confronted by another
sturdy obstacle in the
shape of the
Argentinean Felipe
Contepomi (No.12).

THE MIRACLE MATCH between Ireland and Argentina's Pumas on Sunday 30 September in the Parc des Princes did not, therefore, allow the Irish to save their face in the Rugby World Cup 2007, nor did it enable the French to avoid the All Blacks in the quarter-finals. No miracle occurred in the Parisian stadium, but sporting logic prevailed: the best team in Pool D, dubbed the 'group of death' and undoubtedly the most closely fought of the tournament, had four wins to their credit while conceding only two tries (against Ireland, to be precise). Marcelo Loffreda's Argentineans were the sensation of the first round, thanks to their solid all-round game and their unwavering confidence. They completed an unprecedented clean sweep for countries from the Southern hemis-

Sensational Argentina

The Pumas displayed remarkable assurance in dealing a body blow to France in the opening match and then unflinchingly knocked out Ireland. The Blues, reinvigorated after their initial débâcle, grabbed second place to go through to the last eight.

The eliminated Irish team can only acknowledge the superiority of its Argentinean nemesis.

phere, which came out on top of all their respective pools without registering a single defeat ...

With this faultless trajectory, enhanced by superb tactical intelligence, Agustín Pichot and his comrades showed that their initial win against France on Friday 7 September was no flash in the pan. This historic 17–12 victory was the fruit of strategic, technical and physical virtues. However much the French had stumbled at the first hurdle in the competition, it had to be admitted three weeks later that Argentina's victory had been thoroughly deserved.

The amazing Hernández

The Irish team's opening assaults against the Pumas were stunning as Brian O'Driscoll and his revved-up teammates drove the Argentineans into their own half. It was hard to recognize the uninspired, lacklustre Irishmen who had struggled against Namibia (32–17), Georgia (14–10) and France (3–25). The return of full-back Geordan Murphy undoubtedly breathed new life into the side ... for a whole seven minutes. After this somewhat overheated opening, however, the Irish lapsed into the sorry state that had characterized their earlier matches in the Rugby World Cup 2007.

Magnificently led by its 9–10–12 axis (the trio of Pichot–Hernández–Contepomi), Argentina faltered for a mere quarter of an hour in the face of the Irish onslaught. Two tries from the wings Borges (17th minute) and Agulla (39th minute), 11 points from kicks by Felipe Contepomi and three drop goals from the amazing Juan Martín Hernández earned the Argentineans victory, without really flinching (30–15). The only (slight) regret for the Pumas was that they had been unable to pre-

63

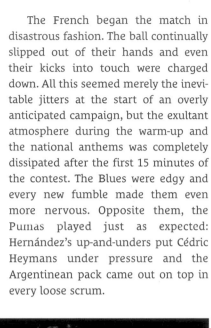

serve their clean sheet as regards tries: a kick charged down by O'Driscoll (32nd minute) and the interception of a long pass by Murphy (47th minute) had momentarily destabilized their hitherto impenetrable rearguard.

The French short-circuit

The wonderful tale of the Pichot posse had begun three weeks earlier under the glare of spotlights in the tournament's opening match against the French in the Stade de France, where the home country's football team had won the World Cup nine years earlier. When Tony Spreadbury, the English referee, blew the final whistle announcing the defeat of Bernard Laporte's men (12–17), he unleashed a kind of national short-circuit. Outside the stadium, and in the 14 million homes that had followed the match live on television, the Blues' supporters were torn between incredulity and despair … After revelling in the bright lights, French rugby was suddenly shrouded in an oppressive darkness, as the country swung from one extreme to the other in just a few minutes.

Supported by an entire nation, by a government that had turned out in force, by the 79,312 spectators in the Stade de France, the French squad, trained by Bernard Laporte – still officially the coach, but already appointed the

Secretary of State for Sport – took a nasty tumble on the first step leading up to a crown that had been imprudently trumpeted as its rightful property. Inflated by their success in the summer against the Welsh and English (twice), by their victory in the 2007 Six Nations Tournament, Raphaël Ibañez and his colleagues had maybe forgotten that there was another form of rugby in the southern half of the planet that had opened up a gap with respect to teams from the Old Continent. This initial failure against the Pumas was made all the worse because it promised – at best – to send 'Les Bleus' into a quarter-final against the All Blacks, and, what is more, away from home, in Cardiff!

The French began the match in disastrous fashion. The ball continually slipped out of their hands and even their kicks into touch were charged down. All this seemed merely the inevitable jitters at the start of an overly anticipated campaign, but the exultant atmosphere during the warm-up and the national anthems was completely dissipated after the first 15 minutes of the contest. The Blues were edgy and every new fumble made them even more nervous. Opposite them, the Pumas played just as expected: Hernández's up-and-unders put Cédric Heymans under pressure and the Argentinean pack came out on top in every loose scrum.

BELOW.
The Pumas celebrate, while Christophe Dominici leaves with his head bowed: a thunderbolt has hit the Stade de France.

ABOVE.
Sébastien Chabal escapes the Namibian Tertius Losper and France breathes again after the stunning blow administered by the Argentineans.

LEFT.
Juan Martín Hernández and the Pumas were behind at half-time against Georgia but went on to defeat the remarkable team spearheaded by 'Irakli Machkhaneli (to the rear).

The Namibian captain Kees Lensing (to the rear) admires the lunge by his team-mate Heino Senekal (No.7) against the Irish star Paul O'Connell.

Christophe Dominici releases the frustration accumulated since the opening match by diving into the Georgian in-goal area.

the emotional aspects at all', admitted the scrum-half Jean-Baptiste Élissalde, a substitute for this match. 'Unconsciously, we thought that things would work out on their own. There was so much emotion on the pitch at the start that we were lost …'

Four days after their initial coup, the Argentineans had to prove their class in the Gerland stadium in Lyon against a Georgian team determined to improve on their baptism of fire in Australia in 2003 (0 classification points and 200 points conceded on the field). Pichot & Co. started the proceedings with a strange mixture of tension and clumsiness against the up-and-unders of the men from the Caucasus. The score was just 6–3 in favour of the Pumas at half-time and it was only 40 seconds before the final whistle that the wing Federico Aramburu scored Argentina's fourth try, thereby entitling his team to an offensive bonus point (33–3).

Ireland in a sorry state

The day before, in the Chaban-Delmas stadium in Bordeaux, the Irish had given a display against the unreliable Namibians that was considered 'very, very weak' by their coach, Eddie O'Sullivan, and 'downright awful' by their fly-half Ronan O'Gara. This may seem a severe verdict for a match won 32–17, but Brian O'Driscoll and his team had managed to lose possession of the ball about 40 times!

Bordeaux also provided the setting for Namibia's match against France. Once the team led by the prop Kees Lensing had recovered from the excitement of their warm reception from

Élissalde: 'We were lost'

In the end, however, the outcome of the duel hinged on small details. In the 27th minute, after a magnificent break by Damien Traille that seemed guaranteed to culminate in a French try, an ill-judged pass by Rémy Martin was intercepted by Horacio Agulla, who set up a killer try for Ignacio Corleto. Right after the interval, a French attack penetrated the Argentinean half only to collapse less than a yard from the try

line (46th minute). There was something pathetic about scrum-half Pierre Mignoni's unrelenting determination as he dispatched his men to crash into Argentina's defensive wall. That night, even the arrival of Chabal, the new favourite of the French supporters, in the 60th minute, proved to be a damp squib. Deprived of the ball and devoid of inspiration, Les Bleus had failed to gain a foothold in a match launched in a blaze of publicity: 'We had not foreseen

ABOVE.
Despite all Ronan O'Gara's efforts, he could not prevent Ireland's sorrowful exit from the first round.

ABOVE RIGHT.
He not only scores (two tries against Ireland), he can also tackle: the French wing Vincent Clerc blocks the huge Brian O'Driscoll.

31,000 cheering spectators, it had to face the reality of France's burning desire to salvage its reputation. The hours following the disappointment of the opening match had given the French squad the chance to put their feet back on the ground and their heads straight. 'Against Argentina, it was 45 who lost,' their captain Raphaël Ibañez had been forced to acknowledge, in reference to the famous '30 of us will win', intended to underline the essential solidarity of the squad. This time, it was the non-playing members who had to face up to their responsibility for the shambles of the opening match of the Rugby World Cup 2007. Backstage, cards were being shuffled.

After the obligatory proclamations of unity, some players were left in reserve and the team's axis was adjusted (Élissalde–Michalak introduced in place of Mignoni–Skrela). All that remained was to reinstil discipline and attacking élan against the Namibian sparring partners. The final score of 87–10 (a historic record for the French team) did not prove much, however, particularly against opposition that was soon reduced to 14 men.

In order to fully redeem themselves and earn a place in the quarter-finals, Les Bleus had to beat Ireland. This challenge turned the France–Ireland game on Friday 21 September in the Stade de France into a 'match of fear' – the fear of being the first host country of a Rugby World Cup to be eliminated from the first round.

A first for Georgia

Finally, the French did win, but with little conviction, and without capitalizing on an offensive bonus point that was theirs

for the taking. Errors were still apparent in every branch of their game, along with a lack of offensive realism and, above all, lamentably slow reactions to attacking balls. There was, however, one rare example of the French flair that had previously been so conspicuous by its absence: a superb kick unleashed from the outside of Fréderic Michalak's foot in the 59th minute that rolled into the Irish in-goal area for the wing Vincent Clerc to touch down. Clerc scored a second try by following up another kick, this time from Élissalde, who also converted five penalties to round off a win for the French with little glory, characterized more by the pack's success in loose scrums and

lineouts than by any attacking brio.

France's last match in the pool, against Georgia in Marseille, was a mere prelude to the decisive Argentina–Ireland encounter. The Caucasus team was exhausted after achieving its Holy Grail just four days earlier by brushing aside Namibia (30–0) and registering its very first win in a Rugby World Cup. The French diligently scored nine tries (64–7) to emerge as the most prolific attacking side in the pool (188 points, 24 tries) – but this did little to shorten their odds a week away from the quarter-final in Cardiff … ■

The Georgians celebrate their historic victory against Namibia 30–0, their first in a Rugby World Cup.

Man of the Pool

THE COMPARISON is so obvious that it is almost a cliché, but it is unavoidable: Agustin Pichot, 5ft 9in, with longish hair, a barrel chest and commanding authority over his pack, is like Napoleon on the battlefield. A man who leads from the front and constantly puts himself at risk. A scrum-half and captain who wants to control everything and gets involved with everybody, without respite. He talks to his players, his opponents, referees, continuously, insistently, in torrents of words that exert pressure and further the designs of 'his' players from Argentina.

A genuine leader of the pack, he is reluctant to elaborate on his leadership of the Argentinean exiles in Europe: 'I'll end up being seen as a Godfather from the Mafia ...' Nevertheless, Pichot is at the forefront of the internationals' revolt against their Federation to demand a form of self-governance within the national team.

Pichot is also a great player who refuses to act the star, a sporting champion who lives in tune with the realities of the

Agustín Pichot is the charismatic leader of an increasingly confident Argentinean team.

67

Agustín Pichot
No.9 in the front line

world. With his brother Enrique, he has formed the Pichot Foundation to help the poor in Argentina, where many foresee a future for him in politics ('the only way to get things moving', in his words). For the last few months, however, the schemer of Buenos Aires had only one thing on his mind: to excel in his third Rugby World Cup as the leader of an Argentinean team that he considers the best he has ever known. In order to spread joy through the streets of Buenos Aires, just as his friend Diego Maradona did in his day, but also to strengthen the case for the Pumas' incorporation into a major international tournament such as the Tri Nations or Six Nations Cups.

Blessed with astute vision and a cool head, the prefect complement to Juan Martín Hernández – his partner at his club Stade Français and the Pumas – Pichot succeeded in leading his men to the quarter-finals against Scotland – with a good chance of going still further and coming up against the Springboks for an extraordinary confrontation, into which he swore to throw himself wholeheartedly: 'Giving everything, you know, that's what makes us proud!'

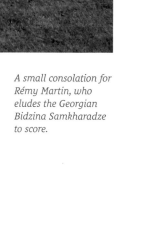

A small consolation for Rémy Martin, who eludes the Georgian Bidzina Samkharadze to score.

The French players (left to right) Cédric Heymans, Clément Poitrenaud, Imanol Hartinordoquy, Serge Betsen (hidden) and Vincent Clerc proudly fly their country's flag in Cardiff after their triumph against the All Blacks.

QF
Quarter-finals

ENGLAND – AUSTRALIA: **12–10**

FRANCE – NEW ZEALAND: **20–18**

SOUTH AFRICA – FIJI: **37–20**

ARGENTINA – SCOTLAND: **19–13**

QF1 QUARTER-FINAL 1
ENGLAND – AUSTRALIA: 12–10

The flowering of the Rose

Australia seemed destined to make short work of an English team that had yet to find their feet – but the title-holders were not ready to relinquish the Webb Ellis Cup just yet. The English pack overran their Wallaby counterparts and Wilkinson's boot put the finishing touches on the first big surprise of the quarter-finals.

MOST COMMENTATORS had ruled England out of the race after their calamitous performance against the Springboks in the pool stage (0–36) but the team made an impressive resurgence in the Rugby World Cup. The title-holders drew on their inner strength to dispatch their Australian 'best enemies' with a mortal blow somewhere between a buffalo charge and the constriction of a boa. Admittedly, their victory in the Stade-Vélodrome in Marseille would never receive any prizes for artistic presentation, but Brian Ashton's men approached the contest with awesome intensity. They overturned all the predictions to trigger off the revolt of the nations from the Northern hemisphere.

Wilkinson overtakes Hastings

To avoid the Australian trap and prevent the Gregan–Barnes tandem from supplying balls to the likes of Stirling Mortlock, Matt Giteau and Lote Tuqiri, the English quite simply brought out their 'weapon of mass destruction', a steely pack of fierce determination led by the captain Phil Vickery. The Wallaby pack went through agony as it collapsed continuously – eight scrums out of fourteen had to be replayed, some up to three times! The Australian movement in the 33rd minute that culminated in a try by Tuqiri, after a new flash of genius from the young Berrick Barnes, could have shaken the English, but their terrifying physical domination continued as before. Despite three failures out of seven, the boot of 'Wilko the Magnificent' was fated to make the difference: twelve penalty points that sealed one of the most important wins in the history of English rugby (12–10). With those twelve points, moreover, Jonny Wilkinson became the highest scorer in the history of the Rugby World Cup with 234 points, overtaking the Scot Gavin Hastings (227 points in 1987, 1991 and 1995).

Catt: 'Everybody had buried us already'

While 'everybody had buried' the English team (in the words of Mike Catt), they had made it to the semi-finals of the Rugby World Cup 2007 and were still in a position to defend the

Andy Gomarsall (aged 33), Jonny Wilkinson (aged 28 but with nine years in the national team), Mike Catt (aged 36) and Jason Robinson (aged 33): England brings out its best veterans against Australia.

title they won four years earlier. The Australians had undoubtedly paid for the dulling placidity of their first round in Pool B, whereas the English, after their humiliating thrashing from South Africa on 14 September, saw themselves as a commando of survivors abandoned, alone, in hostile territory.

'We hate the English!' If John O'Neill, the director of the Australian Federation, had wanted to inflame English passion still further, he could not have chosen a better way of doing it than by making this proclamation, albeit in the tradition of hyperbole that has marked the sporting rivalry between England and its former colony for over a century. In recent encounters between the two countries, the Wallabies have been vulnerable to decisive drop goals: that of Rob Andrew in the quarter-finals of the Rugby World Cup 1995 (victory for England, 25–22) and, even worse, that of Wilkinson, a deadly blow on home ground in the closing seconds of the 2003 final (20–17 in favour of England). High tension was guaranteed for the contest in the Stade-Vélodrome.

The oldest team ever

In order to face up to this challenge, the English coach decided to field the oldest team ever assembled for the Rugby World Cup, with an average age of almost 32 (31 years and 358 days, to be exact). There were fears that Vickery and his cohorts would not be able to stand the pace, but in the end it was the 'youngsters' from the Antipodes who were doomed to experience the worst afternoon of their lives

It took the Irish referee, Alain Rolland, a few minutes to understand what was going on under the scrums – they all had to be replayed up to minute

41 – and he initially penalized the English pack. Mortlock missed two penalties from this source.

After 15 minutes of play, the English went back on the attack and Catt was caught at the last moment by George Gregan. Would the try scored in the 33rd minute – with Barnes in at the beginning (a dummy pass that unsettled the English defence) and at the end (a short ball for Tuqiri, who touched down, 10–6) – allow the Australians to escape from the mire? The answer did not take long in coming, as a rampant Andrew Sheridan immediately led a devastating maul that was thwarted only by a Wallaby foul. Penalty. Wilkinson missed the chance to reduce the gap to one point before the interval.

In his characteristic position, Wilkinson prepares to deal the Wallabies a further blow.

Stirling Mortlock was one of the few Australians who rose to the event, but his devastating raids proved to be of no avail.

The English forwards sweep all before them

After the break, the Australians played their joker by activating their three-quarters. First Mortlock, in the 44th minute, and then Giteau in the 45th attempted to slip through the English defence. That was the moment chosen by the English pack to deliver its *coup de grâce*: a scrum was awarded in Australia's favour, Vickery called for maximum effort and the Wallaby pack reeled back a full two yards with the impact! Unfortunately a knock-on by Catt, served by Wilkinson, prevented a textbook try that could have killed all the suspense of the match at a stroke.

The England team could well have paid for not taking advantage of the breaches created by its steamrolling pack and departed from the Rugby World Cup 2007 that afternoon, a victim of one of the brilliant counter-attacks unleashed by the Wallabies, such as the one in the 53rd minute engineered by Barnes, Giteau and Wycliff Palu, who was finally brought down. The Australian supporters who had joked that the English centres were nothing more than 'swing doors' had to eat their

LEFT.
George Gregan's 139th cap (a world record) had a bitter-sweet taste, as his loyal comrade-in-arms Stephen Larkham was injured and had to end his international career watching from the sidelines.

BELOW.
The English forwards methodically demolished the Australian pack, which was overwhelmed in every scrum.

Jason Robinson's resurrection was even more spectacular than that of his team. His campaign seemed to be over after his injury against the Springboks in the pool stage, but he came back to spread chaos in the Australian defence.

words. Despite the total commitment of the Wallabies, with Mortlock at the helm, the British defence held firm.

Mortlock fails by four inches

In the 61st minute, after another ferocious scrummage from the English (gaining over two yards), the referee awarded a penalty after a foul by the debutant Wallaby flanker Rocky Elsom. Wilkinson converted to take his team into the lead (12–10). The minutes ticked by and the English were at the mercy of another blow of Alain Rolland's whistle. Sure enough, two minutes from the end, the flanker Joe Worsley committed a blatant foul by entering a loose scrum from the side. Stirling

Mortlock was given the chance to snatch victory for his side – albeit a difficult chance of 55 yards, close to the touchline. The Australian centre's kick veered a mere four inches to the left of the English goalposts. The war of nerves in the last few seconds was dominated by Australian attempts to score with their feet. After one final scrum in their favour in the 79th minute, Barnes signalled to Gregan that he wanted to attempt a drop goal, but the ball never came his way. It was the last movement of the match. The steadfast Englishmen gave in to emotion and exhaustion, while the Australians, crouching or sprawled out on the Marseille pitch, seemed stunned, almost incredulous.

Programmed to bring the Webb Ellis Cup back to Sydney, they were taking their leave of the tournament in the quarter-finals!

A tearful farewell for George Gregan

A sad end to the international career of George Gregan, who was bowing out 13 years after his debut, having established a new world record with 139 caps. Like his team-mates, he had fallen victim to the thunderous reawakening of the English team. Phil Vickery's men, absent in body and soul against the United States (28–10) and the Springboks, had 'accepted all the criticism', recovered their metronome,

Wilkinson, and improved with every outing. Refusing to surrender to the depression that had gripped the rest of the country, Rob Andrew, now in the top-level management of the English Federation, had pointed out: 'The Rugby World Cup is not like any other competition. It's got nothing to do with the tournament or test matches. A team has to reach its peak in the last three weeks, not the first three …' In this respect, the English squad regulated its biological clock to perfection. ∎

At the age of 21, the brilliant Wallaby fly-half Berrick Barnes has his whole career in front of him. This was no consolation for being on the receiving end of an English victory.

No drop goals this time for Jonny, although his four penalties instilled panic in the Australian ranks.

Jonny Wilkinson

Jonny will always be Jonny

Man of the match

'WILKO THE MAGNIFICENT' was undoubtedly fated to pay one day for the excessive favours of the rugby gods up to the autumn of 2003 – for having experienced that 'life-changing moment' (in the words of *The Guardian*), that historic drop goal on 22 November 2003 that won England the world title in the final seconds of extra time against Australia (20–17). The price he had to pay turned out to be a high one: 12 injuries and four operations in less than four years.

Obviously, his return to the English fold, on Saturday 3 February 2007, to face Scotland in the Six Nations Tournament, caused a great stir. 'The King is back,' proclaimed *The Sunday Times*. After the match, in which he had scored 27 points (42–20), the star was in relaxed mood: 'It's a great day: I didn't get injured.' Despite a further thigh strain that kept him out of action for four weeks in March, Wilkinson was eager to make up for lost time in France. Then came injury No.13, on 4 September, just four days before the opening of the tournament: an ankle capriciously twisted in a simple training exercise with no physical contact. Once again deprived of the man who 'makes the others play better', England were brittle against America (28–10) and were swept aside by the Springboks (0–36).

The return of the Newcastle fly-half against Samoa brought serenity to the side – as well as 24 points to the scoreboard (44–22). In the decisive match against Tonga (36–20), he needed just one minute – the 19th – to demonstrate that, however much great players suffer, their talent never dies: his diagonal kick to set up a try for Paul Sackey was an expression of pure sporting genius. Jonny Wilkinson's comeback instilled new hope into a whole nation as he scored 52 points in three matches (for a record total of 234 points in Rugby World Cup tournaments) and orchestrated the destruction of the Australian team in the quarter-finals. 'The more Jonny plays, the more effective he will be,' assessed England coach Brian Ashton afterwards – hardly good news for France, his future opponents in the semi-finals.

77

The All Blacks crash into the Maginot line

As in 1999, France shattered the hopes of New Zealand, the hot favourites. There was nothing uncanny on this occasion, however – just a monumental defence and some touches of attacking brilliance. For the first time ever, the last four would not include the All Blacks.

FRANCE – NEW ZEALAND. The long-awaited dream final of the Rugby World Cup 2007, the clash between the host country and the hot favourite, turned out to be just a quarter-final held on neutral territory, in Cardiff's Millennium Stadium – a premature duel resulting from the Blues' unexpected failure against the Argentinean Pumas (12–17). The match was a foregone conclusion for many commentators, mindful of the disappointing French debut, the unimpeded progress of the New Zealanders and the chilling statistics of recent years: the All Blacks have clocked up no fewer than five consecutive wins against the French since the Rugby World Cup 2003, with an overall score of 218–41!

77 per cent possession for the All Blacks

The French, however, ended up coming out on top of the match they supposedly had no chance of winning. The margin was merely two points. Some of the match statistics were truly amazing: 77 per cent possession in favour of the New Zealanders and 197 tackles (178 of

them successful) made by the French! In staunch Gallic style, the Blues had won through their courage and audacity – each player had given his body and soul for the team from the start of a complicated match marked by the KO and withdrawal of Serge Betsen and faulty French kicking. They also won through the depth of their squad and Bernard Laporte's coaching skills: the substitutions that brought on Dimitri Szarzewksi (15 tackles in 28 minutes!) and Frédéric Michalak (who conjured up a try for Yannick Jauzion with his first ball in the 69th minute) proved decisive. The French had said it all along and nobody had believed them: they were going to win this Rugby World Cup, all 30 of them.

A few hours after the English underdogs had toppled the highly rated Australian team, France's qualification for the semi-finals again showed that there was still life in the old countries from the Northern hemisphere.

Oliver: 'A smell of death'

When, in Anton Oliver's words, a 'smell of death' hung over the New Zealand changing room, Graham Henry made an appearance in the French one, which was overflowing with joy. Bernard Laporte requested silence and the Kiwi

Sébastian Chabal, nicknamed 'caveman' during a memorable tour in New Zealand, would emerge as the victor of this particular battle.

coach, impeccable in his squad's colours, swallowed his anguish and uttered five staccato sentences imbued with dignity: 'Congratulations on behalf of the All Blacks. Very well played. Good defence. You deserved to win. Good luck for the rest of the competition!' It is at moments like this that rugby demonstrates its unique qualities!

This unforgettable quarter-final went through so many nail-biting twists and turns that in the end it resembled a slalom more than a rugby match. Who could say exactly which twist of fate was decisive? Maybe the outcome of this exciting contest had been partially decided when the plane bearing the New Zealand delegation had taken off from Auckland on Wednesday 29

August? As the *New Zealand Herald* had proclaimed, the All Blacks had once again departed 'with the burden of the dreams and hopes of an entire nation'. For twenty years the country's rugby fans (i.e. its whole population of 4 million) had been waiting for a world title. When they came face to face with France, even the most robust Kiwis surely found it hard to dismiss from their minds the terrible disappointment of the 1999 semi-final in Twickenham (31–43). On that occasion too, all the experts had written off the Blues. And Jerry Collins was undoubtedly tempting fate when he declared, the night before the match on Welsh soil: 'It will be a long swim home if we don't win ...'

A *haka*, eyeball to eyeball

Maybe another ingredient of this dramatic match was derived from the All Blacks' easy stroll through Pool C, whereas Bernard Laporte's players, having blown their first game, had been obliged from then on to play all their matches on a knife-edge. The quarter-final in Cardiff thus pitted an almost invincible team convinced that, this time, it really was the best, against a group of condemned men afraid to die so far from home.

And then there were the tactical decisions schemed up by the French coaching staff: to keep the New Zealanders in their own half through kicks, to impose pressure in loose scrums to slow down their runs with

the ball and to take advantage of any openings that may arise. This plan would work to perfection, despite shoddy kicking and an unexpected weakness in the lineouts (six throw-ins lost).

Once the squads had passed through the tunnel into the Millennium Stadium, however, the match was no longer in the hands of the coaches but was now the responsibility of the 30 players on the pitch. On the French side, Serge Betsen had come up with a cunning ruse a few days before: to square up to the All Blacks right from the moment of the *haka*, to refuse to be intimidated, just as the English had done against the Tongans eight days earlier in the Parc des Princes.

RIGHT.
Luke McAlister runs too fast for Pieter De Villiers (left), to score the first New Zealand try.

BELOW.
Lionel Beauxis slips, but his penalty from 50 yards sneaks through the goal posts to open the French scoring just before the interval.

LEFT.
Maximum tension! The 22 Frenchmen form a tricolour, eyeball to eyeball with their opponents.

LEFT.
On one of the few occasions when the All Blacks breached the French defensive wall, a tackle by Jean-Baptiste Élissalde (right) stopped Nick Evans at the last moment.

RIGHT.
The turning point: Thierry Dusautoir breaks away, en route to the try that would level the score for France (54th minute).

Throughout the second half, Anton Oliver (with the ball), Richie McCaw (left) and their colleagues concentrated on loose scrums. They broke through only once, however, with a try from So'oialo (63rd minute).

Once the national anthems were over, the 22 Frenchmen unveiled T-shirts specially made for the occasion. They formed a human blue, white and red flag under the noses of Richie McCaw's players and stared into the eyes of their opposite numbers. The sight of these two teams eyeballing each other, without blinking, just a few inches apart, will surely prove one of the lasting images of the Rugby World Cup 2007. The challenge had been thrown down, now the inevitably explosive match could begin.

McAllister, a try and an obstruction

After a few exchanges of long kicks, Raphaël Ibañez and his team hit a bad patch between the tenth and 17th minutes. The All Blacks took advantage of this to score a first try via Luke McAllister, in conjunction with Jerry Collins, only one minute after Vincent Clerc had desperately shoved Collins's feet into touch close to France's goal line. The All Blacks went 10–0 into the lead, then 13–0 after half an hour of play, and it was difficult to see how the French could break free from the Kiwi vice. Lionel Beauxis slipped when taking a penalty from 50m but still managed to convert it, bringing the score to 13–3 and allowing the French to go in for the interval with their spirits slightly raised.

Bernard Laporte took advantage of this new morale to stimulate his men's ambition: '*Allez*, forty minutes left to fight. Forty minutes to a Rugby World Cup semi-final at home, it's worth it, guys!'

After the interval, however, the All Blacks retightened their grip on the match. Byron Kelleher tried to make a run on his own (41st minute) and then

sought assistance from Collins (42nd), but a crushing tackle by Jauzion on McAllister seemed to sow the seeds of rebellion in the French side. In the 46th minute, a French maul advanced 16 yards before being stopped close to the Kiwi goalposts. Élissalde launched an attack to the left for Beauxis, whose kick into the in-goal area induced McAllister to commit an obstruction on Jauzion. The penalty allowed the French to creep up to 13–6 and the New Zealand centre was dispatched to the sin-bin for ten minutes.

The match starts afresh
Even lacking a man, the All Blacks immediately took the battle back into the French half and only a knock-on by Rodney So'oialo prevented them from killing off the match in the 48th minute. Six minutes later, a superb French movement was brought to fruition by Élissalde, Jauzion then Clerc, who allowed the well-positioned Thierry Dusautoir to find the gap between So'oialo and Sitiveni Sivivatu and score the first French try. This gave new hope to the French camp and confirmed the

perspicacity of Bernard Laporte's strategy. Lionel Beauxis's conversion hit the post but went over successfully; 13–13: a new match could begin.

The French, spearheaded by Dusautoir, continued to tackle for all they were worth, always working in pairs – one up front and one further back, to prevent the New Zealanders making fast passes. The slightest error in these circumstances could have dire consequences. So it proved when the Blues lost the ball in a lineout. So'oialo received it six yards from the line, Julien Bonnaire grabbed his ankles in vain and Jérôme Thion flung himself on his back, only to be carried over the line. So'oialo's try took the score to 18–13 in the 63rd minute.

Unbearable suspense
A quarter of an hour remained and the French needed to score again. By now, some of the All Blacks were looking tired. The entrance of Frédéric Michalak in the 67th minute kindled a new spark in this rollercoaster match. When he received the ball for the first time, from an excellent pass (albeit one looking

Brendon Leonard's soaring leap does not deter Frédéric Michalak, on the point of passing to Yannick Jauzion (to the rear) to set up the decisive try.

Four robust All Blacks were not sufficient to obstruct Jauzion, hurtling at full steam towards the New Zealand in-goal area.

LEFT.
The French substitutes hurtle on to the pitch after the final whistle. Their squad, heavily criticized at the start of the tournament, had recovered its pride.

suspiciously forward) from Damien Traille, the Toulouse player avoided tackles by accelerating, then, after being confronted by Joe Rokocoko, sent a superb pass to Jauzion as he keeled over. This second try was converted by Élissalde and the French went into the lead for the first time (20–18).

The closing minutes of the match were unbearable for the supporters on both sides. The Kiwis needed only a drop goal or a penalty to avoid the unprecedented humiliation of being knocked out of the tournament in the quarter-finals. By now, however, the All Blacks had lost both their fly-halves through injury (Dan Carter in the 56th minute then Nick Evans in the 71st) and the saving kick never came. The wonderfully disciplined Blues, heroically resisting the stubborn Kiwi onslaught, continued to make tackle after tackle without committing any fatal foul.

Élissalde takes off

Finally, in the 80th minute, Jean-Baptiste Élissalde picked up the ball and, in an apparent fit of madness, hurtled towards his own half to clear the ball into touch. Wayne Barnes, the English referee, blew the final whistle on this narrow French victory, which sent the Blues into a semi-final against

England in the Stade de France and continued the All Blacks' terrible curse.

Bernard Laporte and his men, severely criticized after their disappointing debut against Argentina, could now return home to pursue their quest for the world title and greet their millions of fans with their heads held high. ■

BELOW.
Jean-Baptiste Élissalde explodes with joy. Vincent Clerc (to the rear) and Damien Traille rush to share his happiness.

Sébastien Chabal and Frédéric Michalak, two substitutes who ended up tipping the scales towards the French team.

Thierry Dusautoir was initially left out of the French squad for the Rugby World Cup – but he ended up scoring one of the most important tries in the team's history.

THIS IS A CLASSIC TALE of the last-minute recruit who changes the destiny of a whole team. Thierry Dusautoir was added to the list of 30 French players as a last resort, following an injury to Elvis Vermeulen: 'At first, the Rugby World Cup in France was just a matter of me and my sofa. When I received the call, I knew straight away that I'd get my chance!'

Thierry Dusautoir

The last-minute comeback

Having made little impact on the international scene prior to the tournament, the flanker from Toulouse made his mark, just short of his 26th birthday, thanks to his extraordinary performance in the quarter-final against the All Blacks. He could not miss this match, after being outclassed in autumn 2006, along with his French team-mates, by the Kiwi pack (3–47). Overwhelmed by the onslaught on that fateful 11 November, he had taken a lot of flak and been truly humiliated in only his third international match: 'I was slaughtered by the press. I was rock bottom…'

The day after his exploits in Cardiff, the Fijian, as he is nicknamed, savoured his revenge: 'They've paid for what they did to me last year. I hope nobody says I was lousy this time …' As the bridgehead in a French pack determined to 'hurt' the All Blacks, Thierry Dusautoir made a record total of 29 tackles and did not blow a single one. The most spectacular was undoubtedly the one in the 26th minute on Jerry Collins, a crashing thump from which the Wellington bruiser took several minutes to recover. And then there was the try that turned the tide, in the 54th minute, that movement which lasted one minute and seventeen seconds – in other words, an eternity – and showed all and sundry that the All Blacks were not invincible.

When the referee blew his whistle to bring the suspense to an end, Dusautoir's first instinct was to keep his distance from the French revelry: 'I was going to go back to the dressing room as usual, but I said to myself, "You're mad, you're not going to have many moments like this in your life."' So, he joined his jubilant colleagues, to share the joy that was originally not destined to be his.

Man of the match

QF3 QUARTER-FINAL 3
SOUTH AFRICA – FIJI: 37–20

The Springboks instil a sense of awe

The South Africans found cannonballs whizzing past their ears when the magnificent Fijians injected a dose of madness into the contest, but the Springboks drew on the power of their pack to become the only major team from the Southern hemisphere still in the tournament.

WHEN THE Fijian players knelt on the grass to salute the 55,000 spectators in the Stade-Vélodrome in Marseille and received a standing ovation in return, it was reasonable to ask how this quarter-final might have turned out if the players from the Pacific had not been deprived of their fly-half Nicky Little, injured in the knee in the last minute of the Wales–Fiji pool match (34–38). There was so little between the teams in this exciting and dramatic quarter-final that this question, although unanswerable, is none the less worth asking.

Pietersen saves the rainbow nation

In the days prior to this third quarter-final, the South African press let its pride go to its head – as so often happens in such circumstances – by suggesting that the Super 14 team from the Western Province should be dispatched to sort out this spot of bother in Marseille … And the centre Jaque Fourie had been unable to conceal his smug self-confidence: 'They're Fijians, you can't take them seriously! Sometimes you have to know how to show a little arrogance. We've got no respect for them!'

Less than an hour after he had scored the first Springbok try (13th minute), Fourie, like all his teammates, was plunged into a crisis of self-doubt by the Fijian onrush. After being reduced to 14 after the temporary expulsion of Seru Rabeni (51st minute) and trailing by 6–20, the 'Flying Fijians' had just scored two tries in two minutes to even the score at 20–20 (Delasau, 57th minute, then Bobo, 59th). Not only that, in the 68th minute, after a superb attack launched by the captain Mosese Rauluni and the wing Vilimoni Delasau, it had required a desperate shove from the powerful South African wing Jon-Paul Pietersen to bring down the Fijian lock Ifereimi Rawaqa by the in-goal area and put the ball into touch.

Bryan Habana, the Springboks' star wing, looks worried in the face of the Fijian onslaught. The pre-match confidence displayed by the South Africans had become frayed.

The decisive moment: Ifereimi Rawaqa was already in the South African in-goal area, all set to put Fiji in the lead, but Jon-Paul Pietersen (right) pushed him into touch at the last moment.

The Springbok forwards assert themselves

The sixth Rugby World Cup was on the verge of witnessing an authentic upheaval: the elimination, within the space of 24 hours, of the three major nations from the Southern hemisphere. After Australia and New Zealand, the Springboks of South Africa were also on the ropes! However, Jake White's men, motivated by their captain John Smit, would dispel all doubts by falling back on their physical strength. Two forceful tries by Juan Smith (70th minute) and Butch James (80th) resulted in a deceptively unequal final score line: 37–20.

Despite the Fijians' visit to the Cathedral of Notre-Dame de la Garde the previous Thursday, no miracle was forthcoming. The stronger and more complete team had won the match, but the Flying Fijians' passage through the Rugby World Cup 2007 will long be remembered.

From the very first moves, there was a sense that all was not well in the South African camp. The young prodigy François Steyn (aged 20) had a particularly troubled spell. In the eighth minute, one of his kicks was knocked down and only a forward pass by the prop Sunia Koto prevented the Fijians from opening the score.

The unthinkable occurs via two tries

The initiatives of the irrepressible Rauluni and Delasau were countered by mauls, with the Springboks focusing

BELOW.
Jaque Fourie scored a try but would have to eat his cocky words before the match.

constantly on their ground play. In the 13th minute, this tactic led to the try by Jaque Fourie, after a long flying pass from the scrum-half Fourie du Preez. The general pattern of the match remained unchanged, however. A break by Rauluni (41st minute) and a kick by Delasau that he himself followed up (44th) sowed panic in the South African squad. The Springboks were looking decidedly nervous.

The match seemed to change course decisively, however, in the 51st minute, when, in a single movement, Ilivasi Tabua's players found themselves

conceding a third try and being reduced to fourteen men after the yellow card shown to Rabeni. Victor Matfield had passed to Pietersen on the wing, who ended up touching down between the goalposts. Fiji faced the last half-hour with a deficit of one man and fourteen points (6–20)!

Then the unthinkable happened. In the 57th minute, Delasau, superbly set up by (yet again) Rauluni, deceived Percy Montgomery and Fourie with a kick that he followed up himself. Delasau beat his opponents to the ball, with the benefit of a very favourable

BELOW.
The umpteenth Fijian surge is held back just a few inches from the line. The Pacific players failed to come up with a definitive knock-out blow against the Springboks.

LEFT
Juan Smith (with the ball) is supported by his imposing pack, which would save South Africa from disaster.

BELOW.
Schalk Burger crashes into Akapusi Qera to get a taste of the famous 'Pacific buffers', the islands' speciality.

bounce, and touched it down. Two minutes later, a devastating double-gear acceleration from Rauluni allowed him to pass to the wing Sireli Bobo, who rolled over the goal line despite a tackle by Du Preez. 20–20 after one hour's play and the crowd in the Stade-Vélodrome was buzzing with excitement.

Smit: 'We were leaking'

After this second try, the South African captain John Smit gathered together his men, who had been scattered over the four corners of the in-goal area by the Fijian parade: 'We were leaking,

losing water,' explained the hooker afterwards. 'I said to them that we couldn't lose, that we were going to make a comeback.' Smit also asked his men to remember the faces of the Wallabies and the Kiwis after their elimination the day before … The speech did not produce any immediate results as Rawaqa almost finished off the Springboks in the 68th minute. Once the Pacific tornado had passed, however, the South Africans recovered their cool and went back to basics, and a text-book maul enabled Juan Smith to cut loose down the left to score in the 70th minute and bring the score to 30–20.

TOP LEFT.
Sirelie Bobo (No.11), the man who runs faster than his shadow, is about to roll into the South African in-goal area to equalize (59th minute).

TOP RIGHT.
The Fijian performance was worthy of a theatre stage. The players saluted the public in the Vélodrome after putting on a magnificent show.

LEFT.
The priceless try scorer Bryan Habana (left) was shaken, like his colleagues, and proved unable to find an opening on that afternoon in Marseille.

White: 'What more could we ask for?'

The match quickly became a contest between hulking forwards. A five-metre scrum for the Fijians was followed by another for the Springboks (76th minute). Three minutes later, after a fourth consecutive try for the South Africans, there was a ferocious battle to expel the ball from a scrum; Butch James eventually came away with it to score the try that took his side to safety (37–20).

Shortly after this complicated qualification, Jake White played down the problems: 'We scored five tries against two, we're in the top four and we're not injured; what more could we ask for?' When he was asked if he'd been scared, he dodged the question: 'People tell me we were lucky not to concede another try … Listen, the number one and two teams have been knocked out! I prefer to be in my shoes today than in theirs …' ∎

Mosese Rauluni
The flying Fijian

Man of the match

HAVING RECEIVED THE ACCLAMATION of the public in Marseille, the captain of the 'Flying Fijians', Mosese Rauluni, was greeted in the press room by the applause of journalists from all over the world. At the age of 32, the powerful scrum-half for the Saracens (5 ft 11 in, 14½ stone) bowed out of the international arena with an exceptional performance. He had been ubiquitous throughout the match against the Springboks, refusing to submit to the law of the strongest, constantly sending his players back to the South African goal line. He was the prime mover in the Fijian challenge, through his involvement in the tries by Delasau and Bobo, as well as the one that Rawaqa failed to score. In the decisive pool match against Wales (38–34), he had already strung together a dazzling series of dummies, sprints and flying passes.

Like most of his countrymen, Raulini was initiated into rugby through playing sevens, and he has preserved an incredible vivacity and unfaltering dexterity from those days. He was strongly influenced by his cousin, the legendary Waisale Serevi, a star of sevens who also participated in three 15-a-side Rugby World Cups for Fiji (1991, 1999 and 2003).

Aware of the happiness that his team had given his 825,000 compatriots ('We've even been told that many Fijians did not go to work the next day because they had celebrated our victories so much'), he did not forget to make a plea for his successors before leaving the stage: 'We have shown that we can compete with the best. But this year we've only played two test matches. To progress further, Fijian rugby needs to face other teams more often …'

Mosese Rauluni tirelessly harassed the Springbok defence to end his international career in fine style.

93

QF4 QUARTER-FINAL 4
ARGENTINA – SCOTLAND: **19–13**

The Pumas make great advances

Argentina, somewhat uneasy in their position as favourites, nevertheless fulfilled all expectations against a misfiring Scottish team. For the first time in their history, the Pumas reach the last four of a Rugby World Cup.

RIGHT.
Once victory had been assured, the highly disciplined Argentineans could permit themselves flights of fantasy, through figures such as Juan Martín Fernández Lobbe, who was triumphant in the Stade de France.

THE FOURTH quarter-final pitting the Argentineans, the best stiflers of play in the tournament, against the Scots, who scraped through Pool C, did not promise to be very spectacular or technically skilful – and it was not. Some of the eliminated teams – Tonga for instance – must have thought, watching the match back home on TV, that luck had really not gone their way …

Although the Argentina–Scotland match may not go down in the annals for its play, it will, however, be remembered for its result: it allowed the Pumas to reach the semi-finals for the first time in their history – an outcome that was thoroughly deserved, given their evolution in the early years of the twenty-first century and their progress in Pool D.

A night of Garryowens
If the truth be told, this contest, long indecisive, was often marked by clumsiness and nerves – the Scottish full-back Rory Lamont was unrecognizable – but this nervousness changed sides after approximately an hour of play. The Argentineans, who until then seemed to

be one step ahead of their opponents, lost their game. Uncomfortable at being favourites, Marcello Loffreda's players knew that 'rugby mania' had erupted back home and that elimination at the hands of the Scots would be hard to explain after the victories in the heat stages against France (17–12) and Ireland (30–15).

Right from the start, the Argentineans applied their customary tactics, with Juan Martín Hernández and Felipe Contepomi trying to make inroads with their kicks. In this respect, they were immediately copied by the Scots Dan Parks and Rory Lamont: the festival of Garryowens, long crosses and attempted drop goals (Hernández missed his first attempt after 17 seconds of play) was under way.

OPPOSITE RIGHT.
With a further penalty and conversion (17 goals scored in all), Chris Paterson (right) maintained his status as 'Mister 100 Per Cent' – but Juan Martín Hernández (left) was one of the nineteen 'Mister Semi-Finals' who took Argentina to heights never before reached in the Rugby World Cup.

The little genius Juan Martín Hernández respected his team's discipline and constantly sent Garryowens up into the skies of the Stade de France.

The Scottish full-back Rory Lamont catches an up-and-under, watched by Ignacio Corleto (right). The Pumas would soon have to change their game plan.

Longo picks the thistle

It was not long before the Pumas unveiled their plan B, however, by dispatching their forwards to conquer Scottish territory. This aggressive strategy bore fruit in the 33rd minute, in the shape of an Argentinean try. The flanker Gonzalo Longo knocked down a clearance from Parks and sprinted into the in-goal area, barely troubled by the wing Sean Lamont. The Argentineans now led by

13–3 and the fumbling Scots seemed unlikely to cause them any problems.

A few kicks later, with the scoreboard now at 19–6 in the Argentineans' favour, Frank Hadden's coaching skills came close to turning things upside down. Three players who came on in the 57th minute were involved six minutes later in the sole Scottish try: a charge from the prop Craig Smith, a pass to the lock Scott MacLeod and a touchdown by the scrum-half Chris Cusiter, which was then converted, after hitting the post, by Mister 100 Per Cent, Chris Paterson (19–13).

Scottish regrets

The last five minutes of the match will long be remembered with regret by Jason White and his colleagues. Edgy and visibly tired, the Pumas conceded the run of the ball to the Scots, who all too often did not know what to do with it. At the final whistle, Agustín Pichot and his team were exultant. The missed opportunities of this quarter-final would soon be forgotten. A semi-final against the Springboks now awaited them, promising to give them back their preferred status as awkward outsiders. ■

ABOVE.
Gonzalo Longo follows up after knocking down a kick from Dan Parks to score the only Argentinean try in the match (33rd minute).

97

Juan Martín Hernández

The industrious artist

Man of the match

THERE ARE NIGHTS like that, when the magicians are less magical, when the artists have to be industrious. For the Argentinean fly-half Juan Martín Hernández, the quarter-final against Scotland was one of those nights. As had been the case since the start of the tournament, 'El Mago' had had to forsake his weaving runs and dummy passes in favour of more mundane up-and-unders. He unreservedly assumed this style that went against his own nature because he believed it marked the Pumas' shortest path to the upper reaches of the competition.

At the age of 25, the versatile full-back from the Stade Français requested a No.10 shirt for the Rugby World Cup 2007. He has all the necessary assets. In the opinion of Felipe Contepomi, 'Hernández is unique; on the pitch he has the elegance of a Zidane!' Ignacio Fernández Madero, Argentina's physical trainer, expresses a similar admiration: 'His ease in space, his strength, his speed, his power, everything is very well balanced.' Elegance, power, speed: a mixture approaching perfection. All that was missing, to score top marks, was a dash of freedom and improvisation ...

Even the formidable Sébastien Chabal (below) buckled under the onslaught of the huge English forwards.

SF

Semi-finals

ENGLAND – FRANCE: 14–9

SOUTH AFRICA – ARGENTINA: 37–13

England shatter the French dream

The English team arose from the ashes at the expense of France. As in 2003, the Blues fell in the semi-finals against their eternal English rivals, who won the right to defend their title in the final.

LEFT.
The final whistle brought relief to the English, exhausted by their fierce but victorious struggle. Jauzion (below) and the French let slip the chance of a Rugby World Cup final at home. An infinite source of frustration.

A WEEK after their triumph against the All Blacks (20–18), the heroes of Cardiff were brought back down to earth: the French rugby players, unlike the footballers of 1998, proved incapable of surpassing themselves in front of a home crowd as soon as the inhibiting role of favourite was thrust upon them.

Without beating about the bush, Frédéric Michalak dealt out a few uncomfortable truths the day after this highly frustrating match: 'Champions are there on day X and, on that particular night, we were not champions,' he explained before regretting the lack of ambition in the French game, based on the occupation of territory through repeated kicks: 'These tactics were valid against the All Blacks as we knew they were dangerous and capable of great feats at the back. While the English are incapable of them …' After the event, many of the French players rued not having dared to have 'played rugby', in the words of Serge Blanco, formerly an outstanding full-back in the national team, with a past record of flashes of inspiration that could change the course

of a match. The 2007 team undoubtedly displayed a cruel lack of leaders like him, capable of steering a ship back on course in the eye of a storm …

Dallaglio: 'Our game plan worked wonderfully'

The French players will have to live for a long time, maybe for their whole lives, with that knot in their stomach reminding them of that night in October 2007, in front of their compatriots. They had had the chance to reach a Rugby World Cup final on home ground and they had let it slip from their grasp through a lack of

courage and lucidity. 'We did not have that extra little bit of soul we had in Cardiff,' admitted Fabien Pelous, banished to the sidelines after a collision with Jonny Wilkinson in the 25th minute. Pelous very quickly felt that this tight match would be decided by 'the toss of a coin that goes the wrong way …'

ABOVE.
This time, the impact players, Sébastien Chabal (left) and Frédéric Michalak failed to bulldoze the French team to victory. The dream of the world title was over.

ABOVE.
The match was barely 80 seconds old when Josh Lewsey dived into the French in-goal area, taking advantage of a fumble by Damien Traille (on the ground). This would be the only try of the match.

PAGE RIGHT, BELOW.
Peter Richards and his colleagues were undaunted by the French barrage of Garryowens and so undermined the Blues' strategy.

As for the English, propelled into the Rugby World Cup final exactly a month after disintegrating against the Springboks in the pool stage (0–36), they still found it hard to believe how little the French team had unsettled them: 'They played exactly as we'd anticipated,' exclaimed the seasoned competitor Lawrence Dallaglio, who came on towards the end of the match. 'Our game plan worked wonderfully …' For the captain Phil Vickery, who once again played superbly at the head of the 'old' English pack, the humiliation of 14 September was part of history. This victory had been achieved by the new England.

Stunning English defence

Totally focused on the task at hand – neutralizing French flair and leaving Wilkinson's boot to finish off the job – Brian Ashton's players had to be extremely realistic from first to last, from Josh Lewsey's try after 80 seconds to Wilkinson's drop goal two minutes from the end. It was undoubtedly this unshakeable confidence in their fly-half that allowed the English to come up with a stunning defensive performance, just as they had done against the Australians in the quarter-finals (12–10).

Brian Ashton's frighteningly efficient 'bulldogs' shattered the French dream. Their resurrection and evolution since the quarter-finals demanded admiration, even though nobody could claim that they were the most thrilling finalists in the history of the Rugby World Cup.

Laporte: 'We blew it'

Bernard Laporte's team found plenty of space available, with the English defence apparently on the verge of collapse every time the Blues finally put together a movement, but, as against the Argentineans (12–17) and the Irish (25–3), there was a glaring absence of any sophisticated attacking game. Had the Cardiff miracle, illuminated by two flashes of brilliance from Thierry Dusautoir and Frédéric Michalak, obscured the reality that the French team had proved deficient throughout the tournament? They had, for example, scored only four tries in their four key matches (Argentina, Ireland, New

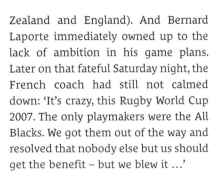

BELOW.
Jason Robinson sowed panic in the French defence and induced a decisive foul six minutes from the end of the match.

Zealand and England). And Bernard Laporte immediately owned up to the lack of ambition in his game plans. Later on that fateful Saturday night, the French coach had still not calmed down: 'It's crazy, this Rugby World Cup 2007. The only playmakers were the All Blacks. We got them out of the way and resolved that nobody else but us should get the benefit – but we blew it …'

Lewsey strikes at the outset

In the opening minutes, the 80,000 spectators in the Stade de France (including over 30,000 English fans) sensed that this duel would be stiflingly tight, as the high stakes involved would smother any creativity. The French fans, however, could barely have imagined a more nightmarish opening than the

string of fouls that led to the try by the English wing Lewsey after only 80 seconds of the game. A French forward pass after the kick-off, a foul by Pieter de Villiers in a scrum, a kick over the defence by Andy Gomarsall, a regrettable hesitation from Damien Traille. As a foretaste of what was to come, the ball bounced up awkwardly to deceive the French full-back, allowing Lewsey to grab it and hurl himself over the goal line. Although the French soon recovered from this disastrous start, these five points, surrendered so quickly, would exert a vital influence on the outcome of the match.

As expected, the battle between the packs was unremitting and Olivier Milloud admitted that Phil Vickery's bruisers had made the French suffer: 'In the lineouts, we were leaking everywhere and, in the scrums, they hit us badly.' All this did not prevent the Blues from having a slight advantage in terms of possession of the ball (53 per cent) and occupation of territory (56 per cent), but this relative French domination served for little.

Even so, the French supporters did have something to cheer about in the 50th minute, when a short kick by Jean-

ABOVE.
Constantly under pressure in the scrums, Jean-Baptiste Élissalde was compelled to try all his tricks, such as this reverse pass demonstrates.

RIGHT.
Although Julien Bonnaire (to the rear) seems to have set up Vincent Clerc (No. 14) for a try, Joe Worsley (No. 19) makes a crucial tackle to stop the French wing just short of the English in-goal area.

Baptiste Élissalde was followed up by Vincent Clerc and Gomarsall was fortunate to manage to push the ball out of play with his right knee. Five minutes earlier, the English had almost scored a second try, when Yannick Jauzion only just managed to catch Matthew Tait. So, the dominance of Raphaël Ibañez and his colleagues was inconclusive, and they remained under threat from a counter-attack.

Ideally served by his forwards, Jonny Wilkinson provides the coup de grace *with his favourite weapon: the drop goal. Thierry Dusautoir (left) and Dimitri Szarzewski (right) are powerless. At 14–9 in the 78th minute, the French team's fate was sealed.*

Clerc stopped by a hair's breadth

There was one splendid touch of French brilliance, in the 68th minute, with a kick from Jauzion to the left wing, then a volley from Julien Bonnaire to Vincent Clerc in full flight, before a lunge by Joe Worsley brought down the French wing. This act of desperation recalled the last-minute tackle by Élissalde on the New Zealander Nick Evans at the end of the match in Cardiff. Once again, the try seemed a foregone conclusion, and, once again, the game was won and lost through a hair's-breadth reaction … On this occasion, Clerc was able to pass the ball to the advancing Sébastien Chabal, but the French impact player was stopped a yard from the line. The ensuing scrum, in favour of the Blues, went their opponents' way. Dimitri Szarzewski dived into the loose scrum and referee Kaplan awarded a penalty to the English. This blow of the whistle, in the 70th minute, sounded a death knell for French hopes.

And a drop goal from Wilkinson …

The rest of the story was predictable. The French had led 9–8 (three penalties by Lionel Beauxis) for half an hour without being able to clinch their advantage. And the situation

that the Blues had managed to avoid against the All Blacks finally arose in the 74th minute: a foul in front of their own goalposts. Put off guard by an outside run from Jason Robinson, Szarzewski grabbed him too high, above the shoulder. An indisputable penalty – and Wilkinson did not miss this opportunity to put his side ahead (11–9). The subsequent French raids were too desperate to surprise the English defence. In the 78th minute, Wilkinson's final drop goal (14–9) merely served confirm the obvious: as in France's quarter-final against New Zealand, victory arguably went not to the better team but to the one that had sought it most astutely. ∎

LEFT.
The jubilant English players savour their victory over their old French rivals and cock a snook at a destiny that seemed to have doomed them a month earlier.

RIGHT.
Phil Vickery has come back so many times (three back operations) that nothing seems able to stop him. Here he brushes the French player Yannick Jauzion out of his path.

BELOW.
Jonny Wilkinson (nine points) was the French nemesis, as in 2003. Here he offers a gesture of consolation to his defeated opponent, Sébastien Chabal.

Man of the match

Phil Vickery
The ideal captain

BRIAN ASHTON CONSIDERED THAT THE MODESTY, courage, stubbornness and intelligence of Phil Vickery made him 'the ideal captain' that England needed for the challenging quest of retaining their world title in France.

The right prop with the Wasps, the winners of the 2007 European Rugby Cup, did not hesitate long last January before accepting the new coach's offer to be the team's route master. At the age of 31, this member of the triumphant 2003 squad had so much experience that nothing new could frighten him. Gruelling farm work had forged both body and soul of this tough man, and even three back operations had done nothing to abate his determination. Not even during the nightmare period of early 2006 when his lumbar vertebra left him in agony: 'The pain was so intense that I had to take a dose of morphine every four hours.' The Cornish hard man had sworn there and then to never give in to suffering; he defied it to the extent of tattooing across his back: 'I'll fight you to the death.'

After the defeat by the Springboks in the pool stage (0–36), Ashton needed the support of his 'Big Tree'. The two men had a private discussion to search for the best way to protect the reigning world champions from the enormous pressure weighing down on them.

When the English side, comforted by the return of Jonny Wilkinson and the win against Tonga (36–20), stood up to the Australian forwards in the quarter-finals (12–10) and their French counterparts in the semi-finals (14–9), Ashton could rely on his spirited 'Raging Bull' to lead the ferocious charges of his old comrades-in-arms from the front.

Barely after achieving success against the Frenchmen led by his friend and club team-mate Raphaël Ibañez, the insatiable Captain Courage was already thinking of the next match – undoubtedly his last – against Os Du Randt and the Springbok pack: 'I wasn't expecting to be in the final, but now that we're there, we have to be worthy of it and make sure that justice is done!'

GENERAL PICHOT and his Argentineans had said repeatedly that they were not content with this place in the semi-finals and intended to continue their triumphal march right to the supreme crown. Trusting in their impermeable defence (only three tries conceded in five matches), the Pumas had begun to dream in their waking hours.

The Springboks on a roll

The exhausted Argentineans were unable to spring another surprise. With their imposing pack and dynamic three-quarters, the South Africans scored four tries to reach the second final in their history.

*PAGE LEFT.
Bakkies Botha, supported by his colleagues, captures the umpteenth lineout throw-in, to the detriment of Gonzalo Longo (right). Superiority in the air was one of the keys to the Springbok victory.*

At the highest level of competition, however, there comes a time when self-confidence and determination are not enough to overcome differences in class. Confronted for the first time in the tournament by a team that was riding high, with dynamic three-quarters and an imposing pack, the Argentineans had to swallow a severe but well-deserved defeat from Jake White's South Africans.

This semi-final, quickly deprived of any real suspense as the Springboks were so evidently superior in every department of the game, provided the occasion for the wing Bryan Habana to score two more tries and equal the record for the number of tries scored in a Rugby World Cup, set by Jonah Lomu in 1999 (eight tries). And as Percy Montgomery decided to imitate the Scot Chris Paterson and play at 'Mister 100 Per Cent' (seven goals from seven attempts), the score sheet at the end was pretty tough on the Argentineans: 37–13 – in other words, the most unequal semi-final since the 45–29 inflicted by the All

*RIGHT.
The superb campaign of Juan Martín Hernández and the Argentineans thoroughly deserved the acclaim of their victors.*

Blacks on England in the tournament hosted by South Africa in 1995.

A South African pack with an average weight of over 18 stone
The run-up to this duel between the 'survivors' of the Southern hemisphere was marked by intense speculation. Which South Africa was going to turn up

on the pitch in the Stade de France? The one that had been shaken by the Fijians in the quarter-finals (37–20), or the indomitable team that had destroyed England in the first round (36–0)? As for the Argentineans, would they be the side that had stifled France (17–12) and Ireland (30–15) in the pool stage, or the one that had struggled to eliminate the

LEFT.
Even the excellent Juan Martín Hernández saw his kicks charged down. The Pumas had reached their limits.

BELOW.
Bryan Habana follows up his own superb kick to fly past Lucas Borges (No.14) to score the first of his two tries of the night.

RIGHT.
Agustín Pichot, hitherto so forceful, was completely neutralized by the South African defence.

Scots in the quarter-finals (19–13)?

The proud Argentineans refused to accept the role of surprise guests at the top table. Their spirits revived by the strategist Agustín Pichot and the bulldozer Rodrigo Roncero, the Pumas refused to be intimidated just 80 minutes away from a place in the final. Although, if the truth be told, the prospect of holding back the 146-stone Springbok pack (an average of over 18 stone per man!) did worry even the sturdiest of the Gauchos: 'We shall have to get the balls out quickly against the Springboks, because in terms of brute strength …' mused Martin Scelzo – not that he himself had

much cause for concern: with a height of 6 ft 3 in, he tips the scales at 19½ stone.

Argentina crack mentally

The Pumas, who had displayed admirable tightness since the start of the tournament, proved unable to keep up with the rhythm established by John Smit and his team right from the start. It was the mentality of Marcelo Loffreda's men, rather than their legs, that seemed to give way. Edgy from the outset, forgetting the virtues of discipline that had brought them this far, the Pumas committed one blunder after another.

On Sunday 14 October, however, in the face of Fourie Du Preez, armed with a battery of powerful rockets by the name of Bryan Habana, Jaque Fourie, François Steyn and Jon-Paul Pietersen, the Argentineans could not afford to make any mistakes. But, feeling the pressure very early on, they made at least four – four fatal errors (in the seventh, 32nd, 40th and 76th minutes) that the Springboks immediately pounced on.

The Pumas are not immune to clumsiness

The Pumas, who had avoided opening

themselves up too much since the start of the Rugby World Cup 2007, had apparently decided to attack more uninhibitedly in this semi-final in order to make the powerful South Africans run. And run they did! In the seventh minute, a pass from Felipe Contepomi was intercepted by Du Preez, who sprinted 85 yards to score the first try of the match. In the 32nd minute, after the ball was retrieved by Schalk Burger, a long flying pass from Steyn allowed Du Preez to supply Butch James, who set Habana on his way. The lightning South African winger kicked the ball, followed it up himself and outran both Horacio Agulla and Manuel Contepomi to make the score 17–6. Nevertheless, the match was still within reach of the Argentineans, but just a few seconds before the interval, a handling error by Juan Martín Hernández – a long knock-on 25 yards in front of his goalposts, a mistake as unusual as it was inept – put the ball into the hands of Steyn. A powerfully propelled pass from Burger set up a try for the flanker Danie Rossouw.

The Springboks dominate the lineouts

With a score line of 24–6 at half-time, the result seemed a foregone conclusion. Not so much because of the score but because of the extent of the South African domination. Noticeably outclassed in the lineouts by the imperious trio of Victor Matfield–Bakkies Botha–Juan Smith (eight balls stolen from Argentinean throw-ins), Pichot's team was unable to compensate for such deficiencies.

After the break, however, the Springboks gave the impression of suffering in loose scrums and, after the Argentineans poached the ball in the South African half, Pichot supplied it to Hernández, whose flying pass sent Manuel Contepomi on his way to a try (45th minute). More so as the Pumas inexplicably opted not to attempt the conversion of a penalty, awarded to them in the 60th minute, that would have brought them to within eight points of South Africa.

Mario Ledesma (with the ball) is threatened by the Springbok forwards Schalk Burger (left) and C.J. Van der Linde (right).

Not only that, they started to flag physically at around this point, and two further penalties against them allowed the unflappable Montgomery to take the score to 30–13.

The gift season

The gift season was still not over, however, as a hesitant pass from Hernández to the substitute centre Gonzalo Tiesi was stolen by Bryan Habana, who charged off, with a smile on his face, to score his eighth try of the tournament. Montgomery's conversion took the final score to 37–13.

The Argentineans, brutally brought back down to earth, had to console themselves with a place in the 'bronze final' against France in the Parc des Princes, while the South Africans, more confident than ever, could quietly prepare for the real final in the Stade de France and plot their revenge against an English team that definitely did not frighten them …■

Danie Rossouw (left) is awed by the talent of Bryan Habana, who equalled Jonah Lomu's record for Rugby World Cup tries: 'In his case, the magic can come at any moment!'

Bryan Habana
The electric cheetah

Man of the match

WHETHER TEARING THROUGH defences in the Super 14 or the Tri Nations Cup, or challenging a cheetah in a sprint on a dusty track in a South African nature reserve (in benefit of a wildlife protection foundation), Bryan Habana is one of the stars of YouTube, the famous video-sharing website. Whether jumping on the slightest mistake or rushing to pursue an attacking kick, the Pretoria Bull left wing electrifies his enemies and accumulates spectacular tries.

Having never been a member of even a provincial athletic team, Habana admits that he has had to work long and hard to develop his speed. Explosive and unpredictable, he continues, at the age of only 24, to astonish his fellow Springboks: 'In his case, as soon as he gets the ball, even if there's no apparent danger, the magic can come at any moment!' enthused Danie Rossouw.

Almost embarrassed by the compliments, Habana is content to thank 'the Man up there', the God who has 'given him talent'. Without entering too far into a political arena close to his heart, the mixed-race player brought up in the more sheltered neighbourhoods of Johannesburg is quick to declare his admiration for Chester Williams, who, like him, wore the No.11 shirt for the Springboks and was the only black player in the world champion team of 1995.

After an uneven 2006–07 season, Bryan Habana came back to form in spring in the last matches of the Super 14, particularly in May, when he proved decisive in a 100 per cent South African final between the Bulls and the Durban Sharks (a try in the 80th minute for a 20–19 victory). Then, on 9 September in the Parc des Princes, the Springbok wing burst into the Rugby World Cup 2007 by scoring four tries against the Samoans (59–7). After being showered with gift opportunities by the Argentineans, Habana had another field day in the semi-finals, with two further tries that brought him level with Jonah Lomu in the table of try scorers in the Rugby World Cup, with eight tries – and hopefully more to come, including a possible world title on 20 October in the Stade de France. And, above all, his most cherished dream, that of becoming the Springboks' first mixed-race captain.

113

The entire Argentinean family gathers around Agustín Pichot (centre) to celebrate their third place, the best result in the history of the Pumas.

3rd

Third-place play-off

ARGENTINA – FRANCE: **34–10**

The Pumas finish off France

By scoring five tries, Argentina confirmed their superiority in the opening match in devastating style, while the Blues finished 'their' Rugby World Cup on a sad note.

Sébastien Chabal is foiled by the implacable Puma defence, watched by David Skrela (left) and Alberto Vernet Basualdo.

BY SUCCUMBING to Argentina 10–34 and conceding five tries in the Parc des Princes, the French proved that a rugby team can die twice in one week. On Saturday 13 October in the Stade de France, the Blues missed the chance of a lifetime by faltering in the semi-final against England (9–14). On Friday 19 October, half a dozen miles away, Raphaël Ibañez and his men were forced to make their exit with their heads down.

Laporte: 'The best side won'

In the turbulent first half-hour of play, the French attack tried time and time again to bypass the South American defensive wall, but in vain. Moreover, France's unsuccessful attempts to advance left them vulnerable to the kings of the counter-attack, in the shape of Ignacio Corleto, Juan Martín Hernández and the Contepomi brothers. The unevenness of the match may have seemed unfair at times, but there was no disputing the result of this master class: 'The best side won. They have beaten us twice in this Rugby World Cup, we're behind them, that's obvious,' admitted Bernard Laporte. The Pumas had beaten the Blues for the sixth time in seven contests, and to top it all they had obtained their widest margin (24 points) against this side!

As they climbed on to the podium to receive their bronze medals, Agustín Pichot and his Argentinean squad were jumping around like little kids. They had managed to draw deep on their resources to keep themselves together as a team, overcoming their disappointment and concluding their collective campaign on a high. 'That was really a wonderful adventure,' enthused the prop Omar Hasan. 'There'll never be anything like this squad again.'

An unstoppable counter-attack

Right from the kick-off of this 'mini-final', the French threw themselves energetically into their siege of the Argentinean fortress. In the 25th minute, a kick from Frédéric Michalak found Rougerie on the edge of the Argentinean in-goal area, but the ball landed on the French wing's shoulder and Felipe Contepomi neutralized the threat. Then the Blues fell victim to a dazzling, unforgiving and totally unstoppable counter-attack. A blind-side break by Pichot bamboozled the French defence and Felipe Contepomi (him again) effortlessly rounded off the movement (28th minute).

Four minutes later, following an attempted drop goal from Hernández that hit the right goal post and bounced back into play, Jean-Baptiste Élissalde was caught off guard. The Argentinean pack pounced on the opportunity and Hasan stormed over the goal line.

Ibañez in the sin-bin

17–3 in favour of the Pumas. A cruel score sheet for the French, but one that could not be attributed merely to bad luck as Laporte's players were uninspired and made many mistakes. In the 37th minute, when a promising French maul emerged just three yards from the Argentinean in-goal area, Nyanga went off on his own to the right, to try his luck alone, only to impale himself on the Pumas' defence …

The next five minutes were played out within the Argentinean 22-metre line, with three penalties going the French way five metres from the line – to no avail! An exasperated Raphaël Ibañez ended his third and last Rugby

*Agustín Pichot
launches an
Argentinean attack,
watched concernedly
by Frédéric Michalak.*

World Cup in sorry fashion by flagrantly stamping on Rimas Alvares-Kairelis in a loose scrum. Referee Honiss sent off both players for ten minutes.

The Corleto flash-back

The second half evolved along similar lines: in the 53rd minute, the Blues faced another counter-attack. Corleto sowed panic in the French defence and set up a further try for Federico Martin-Aramburu. With the score at 22–3, the game was turning into a nightmare for the French. More was to follow, however: when Vincent Clerc lost a ball in attack, Horacio Agulla sent Corleto on his way for the fourth Argentinean try (65th minute). The Argentinean full-back's acceleration left Christophe Dominici rooted to the spot – a painful flash-back to the French defeat on 7 September.

Michalak's ice pack

Poitrenaud's try (69th minute) softened the blow slightly, although it prompted a second try from Felipe Contepomi, from a pass by Nicolas Fernandez-Miranda – taking the final score to 34–10.

On the fringes of the Argentine celebrations, the French undertook a slow lap of honour, their eyes brimming with tears. Michalak was holding an ice pack to his head – like him, the entire French rugby establishment left the Rugby World Cup with a terrible headache! ■

Just as Nelson Mandela and François Pienaar had done in 1995, the black president of the Republic of South Africa, Thabo Mbeki, shares the joy of the Springbok world crown with their white captain, John Smit, seen holding the Webb Ellis Cup.

F

Final

SOUTH AFRICA – ENGLAND: 15–6

The key to the South African triumph in a single image: dominating forwards like Bakkies Botha (left) providing service for backs overflowing with talent, with the centre Jaque Fourie (right) and, above all, an exceptional finisher, Bryan Habana, who is deservedly borne aloft in triumph.

The Springboks, a foregone conclusion!

After a final with no tries, South Africa disposed of England to capture their second world title – a just reward for their power and constancy throughout the tournament.

A hug from Martin Corry cannot console Jonny Wilkinson. England has lost their world title.

JAKE WHITE, often accused of arrogance because of his remarks prior to the tournament, was savouring his Springboks' triumph on Saturday 20 October 2007. What had the South African coach been saying over the course of that year's summer? Two very simple things: that the world title would go to the team with the best defence, and that that team would be South Africa.

And it has to be admitted that White was right on both counts. South Africa were the most disciplined team of the tournament, with the tightest defence of the four semi-finalists (only 86 points conceded in seven matches) to grace the pitch in the Stade de France. Moreover, the draw had enabled them to avoid confrontations with both New Zealand and Australia. The Springboks, the only team undefeated in the Rugby World Cup 2007, came out on top of a competition after gliding over it, troubled only by a few minutes of turbulence two weeks earlier against the Fijians (37–20)

that saw John Smit's team, hitherto so intractable, concede two tries in two minutes and Jon-Paul Pietersen desperately prevent a third that would have put Fiji into the lead.

Solid and talented at the back, robust and enterprising up front

All that remained was for the South Africa–England final, short on spectacle and lacking in tries, to consecrate a Springbok team as solid and talented at the back as it was robust and enterprising up front. Which other team could boast of wings like Bryan Habana (the tournament's best try scorer, with a total of eight) and Pietersen, or a full-back and goal scorer as unruffled as Percy Montgomery (highest scorer with 105 points), or a scrum-half as decisive as Fourie Du Preez? Which other side could call on a pack to match the awesome back row of Schalk Burger–Danie Rossouw–Juan Smith, the imposing second-row tandem of

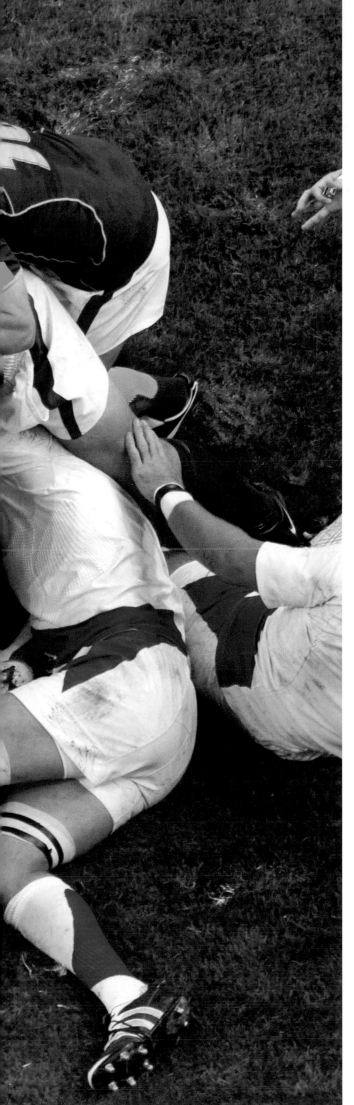

The fierce battle of the forwards went ahead as expected on the pitch of the Stade de France. Unfortunately for the English, they showed less discipline than in their matches against the Australians and the French.

Bakkies Botha–Victor Matfield or a cornerstone as reliable as the hooker and captain Smit?

The result seemed a foregone conclusion, especially as the English, who had experienced an astonishing renaissance that month, could not fully exploit the brilliance and kicking skills of Jonny Wilkinson in the final, and, furthermore, witnessed the loss through injury of Jason Robinson, their other unnerving genius, in the 44th minute.

South Africa draw level with Australia

The Springboks came out on top of the sixth final of the Rugby World Cup without really being troubled, watched by the president of the Republic of South Africa, Thabo Mbeki, the successor to Nelson Mandela. Their low-scoring victory (15–6) allowed the 'Rainbow Nation' to join Australia in the exclusive club of countries that have been world champions twice, and Os Du Randt, the only survivor from 1995, to become only the fourth player to enjoy this honour.

The memory of the match in the pool stage on Friday 14 September (South Africa–England, 36–0) obviously hung over the Stade de France. Five weeks earlier, in the very same stadium, the Springboks had destroyed a soulless English team. Jake White's side had to avoid any complacency, while England had to remember the collective revival that had followed that disaster and maintain one of the most extraordinary comebacks in the history of rugby.

A stadium shrouded in white

As was to be expected, the Stade de France was shrouded in white. 'Swing Low, Sweet Chariot' kindled the dreams of the English fans – dreams that seemed unthinkable just a month before. It very quickly became obvious that the night would be dominated by high

balls, with the Garryowens of Wilkinson, Robinson and Mike Catt countered by those of Montgomery, Butch James, François Steyn and Du Preez.

In the seventh minute, the match gave the lie to recent statistics. In the three previous Rugby World Cup finals, the team that scored first had ended up losing. Now, however, Matthew Tait was penalized for holding the ball on the ground after the collapse of the English scrum. The penalty, in front of the goal-posts, was a gift chance for Percy Montgomery to open the scoring (3–0).

The English handicapped by fouls

This was the first major English foul and by no means the last. On a further four occasions, Phil Vickery & Co. offered easy points to the boot of the

Yet again, a left-footed goal scorer made a decisive impact on the final. Percy Montgomery punished English errors mercilessly.

Jonny Wilkinson, the hero of Sydney, was unable to extract himself from the trap set by the Springboks.

South African full-back or, for longer distances, that of François Steyn (at the age of 20 years, five months and six days, the youngest ever participant in a Rugby World Cup final).

A trip by Lewis Moody on James (16th minute), a side approach to a loose scrum, from Moody yet again (40th), a ball played on the ground by Martin Corry (51st) and a screen by Ben Kay (62nd). Five fouls, five penalties and fifteen points for the Springboks. The English, who had been so disciplined since their resurrection against Tonga (36–20), were accumulating an almost insurmountable handicap.

Jones: 'A real battle'

After half an hour of already very tough play, the match acquired an extra intensity. A counter-attack by Jason Robinson was stifled only with difficulty (26th minute). The South Africans' reaction was stunning: Steyn set off on an astonishing slalom before being stopped by Wilkinson (36th minute). The commitment on both sides was unrelenting, particularly in the rucks: 'It was a real battle,' concluded Eddie Jones, the Australian coach, now a technical consultant for the South African squad.

The clash of the forwards gave way to headlong runs. After a boisterous English scrum that was eventually awarded to the South Africans by Alain Rolland, the referee, a charging surge by Danie

Rossouw was blocked just a few feet from the line, but Moody was penalized for a foul in the subsequent loose scrum. Brian Ashton's players were lucky to get away with conceding only three points.

Cueto, foiled by the video referee

Two minutes after the interval, the outcome of the final seemed to revolve round a matter of inches. Matthew Tait surprised first Steyn, then Jaque Fourie and Montgomery. The action veered

42nd minute: Mark Cueto (right) touches down, despite a desperate charge by Danie Rossouw. A try? No, as the video replay would show that the English wing's foot had clipped the touchline.

towards the left wing: Mark Cueto received a volley from Wilkinson and dived over the line, resisting a charge from Rossouw. Unfortunately for the English, the impact of the Springbok had been sufficient to deflect the lower half of Cueto's body. The video recording was examined long and hard. It resulted in the overruling of the try, as Cueto's left foot had been in contact with the touchline. The referee gave England the advantage and awarded a penalty, which was converted by Wilkinson with

a kick that bounced off the goalposts: 9–6, and all was not lost for England.

In the 44th minute, however, more bad luck befell the title-holders. Jason Robinson received a heavy blow on the shoulder and was forced to go off, although this did not discourage the English from continuing in the same implacable fashion.

The Springboks, masters of the air

Contrary to expectations, however, the

match would not be decided in closed scrums but in the battle of the air. And, as had been the case since the start of the tournament, the Springboks soared above the opposition (with Matfield particularly extraordinary!) by capturing seven balls from 26 English throwins in the lineout. At 15–6, with just over ten minutes remaining, one of these lineouts turned out to be crucial. Wilkinson sent a penalty into touch ten yards from the South African line: George Chuter's throw-in passed over

Corry, Juan Smith beat Joe Worsley to the falling ball and James let the Springboks off the hook by booting it way into touch ...

In the last ten minutes, England tried everything their flagging bodies would allow, seeking inspiration in a new burst of energy from Wilkinson (although he had an off day and missed two drop goals). In the 80th minute, Fourie Du Preez kicked the ball into touch with all his might and the Rugby World Cup was all over.

One people, two trophies

While the last 'a' of South Africa was being engraved on to the gilded base of the Webb Ellis Cup, the English were sadly receiving their silver medals. Phil Vickery compared his bulldogs' adventure to a 'rollercoaster', insisting that he had really believed in their ultimate victory but admitting that 'the Springboks deserved their title of world champions'. Then it was the turn of John Smit and his players to climb on the podium and brandish the trophy, alongside their president Thabo Mbeki, who was soon borne aloft in triumph with the Webb Ellis Cup in his arms ... Twelve years after the apotheosis of 1995, the South Africans in the stadium could dance and sing, celebrating their second world title with a giant maul that bore new hopes! ∎

Yet another high ball captured by Victor Matfield and the South African second row, the undisputed masters of the lineout throughout the tournament.

The highest scorer of the tournament, with a total of 105 points: Percy Montgomery has every right to brandish the Webb Ellis Cup, a trophy with the lustre of personal vindication.

THROUGHOUT THE WEEK prior to the final, the British tabloids had made fun of the immaculate blonde hairdo of Percival Colin Montgomery, even going as far as to liken him to a 'peacock'. 'Monty the Surfer' was unperturbed, having revelled in a reputation for eye-catching style ever since his international debut in June 1997 against the British Lions. Even though he may look as if he's just sauntered out of the bathroom when he emerges from a brutal ruck, 'Beautiful Monty' is not the type to shy away from physical contact. The

Percy Montgomery
Beautiful Monty

Man of the final

Springbok full-back – faultless under the Garryowens of Wilkinson and Catt, unyielding in defence for 80 minutes, unruffled when a push by Toby Flood sent him tumbling on to a TV cameraman behind his in-goal area – earned the distinction of scoring four crucial penalties in the final. With 105 points in seven matches, he was the highest scorer of the Rugby World Cup 2007.

Born in Walvis Bay in Namibia 33 years ago, Percy Montgomery had seemed destined never to participate in a second Rugby World Cup after his five matches in the 1999 tournament. In early 2002, 18 months before the Rugby World Cup in Australia, his style annoyed many South African supporters and he did not figure in the plans of the new coach Rudolf Straeuli. Tired of receiving whistles and pejorative comments about his appearance, he decided to leave the country to join the Newport Dragons in Wales: 'I worked hard there and I was judged by the quality of my play, not the length of my hair!'

Two years later, however, Jake White – impressed by the professionalism of a player whom he considered had been 'criticized unfairly' – recalled Montgomery as an integral part of the victorious team in the 2004 Tri Nations. The following year, Monty returned to South Africa and signed up with the Natal Sharks, although he went back into exile for the 2007–08 season, to play for Perpignan in the Top 14.

When Monty beat Joost Van der Westhuizen's record for appearances with the Springboks in the match against Tonga (30–25), this was only the most recent of several ground-breaking feats: last August he beat the national record for the number of points scored in a test match (35), against Namibia (105–13), while already holding the records for conversions and tries. With a total of 876 points to his credit in 94 matches for the Springboks, the new arrival in Perpignan could be tempted to prolong his stay in the team to pass the mythical barriers of 100 caps and 1,000 points. At the age of 33, he feels there is still life in him and attributes his longevity to a simple formula: 'I keep my mouth shut, I eat well and I drink red wine!'

127

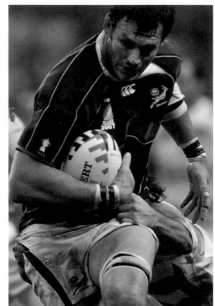

kinstad Jannie **DuPlessis** John **Smit** Os **DuRandt** Bakkies **Botha** Victor **Matfield** Schalk **Burger** Juan **Smith** Danie **Rossouw** Fo

uPreez Butch **James** Bryan **Habana** François **Steyn** Jaque **Fourie** Jon-Paul **Pietersen** Percy **Montgomery** Jake **White**

PORTRAITS
of the champions

The Webb Ellis Cup won by Jake White's Springboks was split 32 ways: all the players in the squad went on to the pitch at least once in the Rugby World Cup 2007, including Wayne Julies and Jannie Du Plessis, who were called up during the tournament after injuries to Jean De Villiers and B.J. Botha. Every one of them is a world champion, although a first-choice team of fifteen, with a heavy emphasis on impact players, clearly emerged from the quarter-finals onwards.

The flanker Juan Smith, seen here scoring against England in the pool stage, proved himself as one of the key elements in Jake White's strategy.

John **Smit**

HOOKER (CAPTAIN)

Born 03/04/1978

6ft 6in, 18st 3lb

Club 2007–08: Clermont (FRA)

74 apps, 4 tries

RWC 2007:

7 matches, 1 try

Against all the odds, Jake White chose Smit as his captain for both the under-21s in 2002 and for the Springboks. He received this ultimate honour in June 2004 and two years later he was instrumental in the South African team's first triumph in the Tri Nations since 1998. Smit's motto is: 'It's good to be somebody important but it's important to be somebody good!' With 74 caps and 48 tests to his credit as captain (taking him past the record of 36 captaincies held by his role model Gary Teichman), he has now taken his place in the pantheon of South African rugby alongside François Pienaar, the captain of the epic 1995 campaign. In 2007–08, Smit will play for Clermont in the French Top 14.

Percy **Montgomery**

FULL-BACK

Born 15/03/1974

6ft, 13st 12lb

Club 2007–08: Perpignan (FRA)

94 apps, 873 pts
(24 T, 145 P, 6 D, 150 C)

RWC 2007:

7 matches, 105 pts
(2 T, 17 P, 22 C)

The former full-back for the Natal Sharks was dropped from the Springbok team between November 2001 and June 2004, during his exile in Wales, but he went on to become one of the key players in Jake White's calculations. With his total of 105 points (top scorer in the tournament) and a reassuring constancy with his kicking (four out of four goals in the final against England), the much maligned Monty made his detractors eat their words. He proved to be one of the Springboks' most resolute defenders, staunchly catching the up-and-unders relentlessly launched by first the Argen-tineans (in the semi-final) and then the English (in the final). His 94 games for the national team (with 873 points, another record) make him, at the age of 33, the most capped player in South Africa's history.

E: Try ; **C:** Conversion ; **P:** Penalty ; **D:** Drop goal.

Jon-Paul **Pietersen**

WINGER

Born 12/07/1986

6ft 3in, 13st 5lb

Franchise 2007: Sharks

15 apps, 6 tries

RWC 2007:

7 matches, 4 tries

At the age of 23, the powerful Natal Shark is Bryan Habana's counterpart on the right wing for the Springboks, and he is undoubtedly somewhat over-looked by the media as a result. J.P. Pietersen (J.P. in homage to the famous Welsh full-back J.P.R. Williams) summoned up a great performance against England in the pool stage (two tries), but he had established himself as suitable material for Jake White's strategy only in the spring of 2007. With four tries, he was the second highest score in the world champion team (tying with Jaque Fourie and Juan Smith). He will be most remembered, however, for his crushing tackle on the imposing Ifereimi Rawaqa (6 ft 6 in, 18 stone 12 lb), which avoided an upset for the Springboks a quarter of an hour from the end of their quarter-final against Fiji.

Jaque **Fourie**

CENTRE

Born 04/06/1983

6ft 2in, 15st 1lb

Franchise 2007: Lions

37 apps, 20 tries

RWC 2007:

6 matches, 4 tries

After recovering from injury in the autumn of 2003, this April Lavigne fan was surprised to find himself in Rudolf Straeuli's squad for that year's Rugby World Cup, where he made his debut – and scored his first try – in the green-and-gold shirt at the age of 20, playing at centre, in the Springboks' rout of Uruguay (72–6 and twelve South African tries). Since then, Fourie has also acquitted him-self well in defence and has accumulated 37 caps, with a total of 20 tries, including four in this Rugby World Cup 2007 (one against Samoa, two against the United States, one against Fiji) – making him the second highest scorer of tries, along with J.P. Pietersen and Juan Smith.

A tireless tackler, forceful in attack and adept in the lineout, Danie Rossouw enjoyed an excellent Rugby World Cup and, above all, a splendid final against England.

François **Steyn**

CENTRE

Born 14/05/1987

6ft 3in, 15st 10lb

Franchise 2007: Sharks

16 apps, 41 pts
(4 T, 4 P, 3 D)

RWC 2007:

7 matches, 17 pts
(1 T, 4 P)

At the tender age of 20 years, five months and six days, François Steyn became, on 20 October 2007, the youngest player to participate in a Rugby World Cup final – a heavy burden for this versatile artist, equally comfortable in shirts with numbers from 10 to 15 and endowed with an ideal build (6 ft 3 in, 15 stone 10 lb). He showed signs of nervousness against Fiji in the quarter-finals, as well as in the semi-final against Argentina, but his foot did not waver when, after an hour's play, he had the chance, from a distance of 52 yards, to bring the score to 15–6 against England in the final. In only his fourth match for the Springboks, in the 2007 Tri Nations, he took them to victory against Australia in the last six minutes through two daring drop goals.

Bryan **Habana**

WINGER

Born 12/06/1983

5ft 10in, 14st 6lb

Franchise 2007: Bulls

35 apps, 30 tries

RWC 2007:

7 matches, 8 tries

The 24-year-old left wing from the Pretoria Bulls has been the crowning glory of the South African attack for three years, since the first try he scored in Twickenham in November 2004, in his very first match. Nicknamed 'Speedy Habana', he continues to surprise opposing defences with his explosiveness and instinct for interceptions. With eight tries scored in seven matches, he equalled the record established by Jonah Lomu in the Rugby World Cup 1999. Just as decisive in 2007 with his club (contributing to the first South African triumph in the Super 14) as with the Springboks (13 tries in ten matches), Bryan Habana also demonstrated in the final against England that he is equally adept in defence.

Butch **James**

FLY-HALF

Born 08/01/1979

6ft 1in, 15st 3lb

Franchise 2007: Sharks

26 apps, 61 pts (3 T,
12 P, 5 C)

RWC 2007:

6 matches, 9 pts (1 T, 2 C)

The fly-half for the Sharks embodies the slightly less golden aspects of the Springbok story. In November 2002, his international career went on ice after the débâcle in Twickenham (3–53 defeat). His wilderness years were blighted by two knee operations and it was not until July 2006 that Jake White recalled him to the position of fly-half. This explains why, at the age of 28, he has only 26 caps. Lacking in flair (but also in any glaring flaws), the sturdy No.10 scored his fourth international try in the 80th minute of the quarter-final against Fiji, thereby bringing deliverance to the Springboks.

Fourie **Du Preez**

SCRUM-HALF

Born 24/03/1982

6ft, 13st 12lb

Franchise 2007: Bulls

37 apps, 9 tries

RWC 2007:

6 matches, 2 tries

Voted South African player of the year in 2006, the Springboks' scrum-half forms part of the 'Jake White generation': it was under White's command that he became a member of the under-21 world champion team in 2002. The son of the former Northern Transvaal flanker Fourie Du Preez Sr and nephew of the former Springbok lock from the 1960s Frik du Preez, the 25-year-old No.9 for the Pretoria Bulls enjoyed an exceptional season in 2007, first as a winner of the Super 14 with his club, then as an astonishingly mature playmaker for the Springboks. Inspired and unpredictable in attack, solid in defence, impeccable with his feet, Fourie Du Preez is undoubtedly the best scrum-half in the world.

Danie **Rossouw**

FLANKER / NO.8

Born 05/06/1978

6ft 6in, 18st 8lb

Franchise 2007: Bulls

31 apps, 6 tries

RWC 2007:

6 matches, 1 try

Danie Roussouw, capable of playing in the back row or as a lock (where he was outstanding in tests against Scotland in June 2006), is distinguished by a speed that is extraordinary for a man of his size (6 ft 6 in, 18¾ stone). It was Roussouw who, in the 42nd minute of the final, summoned up a desperate tackle that deflected the lower body of Mark Cueto sufficiently for the left foot of the English wing to graze the touchline before touching down. Like Jaque Fourie, this powerful player from the Pretoria Bulls made his Springbok debut against Uruguay in the Rugby World Cup 2003, when he also scored his first try.

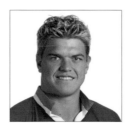

Juan **Smith**

FLANKER

Born 30/07/1981

6ft 4in, 16st 9lb

Franchise 2007:
Cheetahs

41 apps, 9 tries

RWC 2007:

7 matches, 4 tries

Although less spectacular than 'Hulk' Burger, Smith is the type of dogged battler that any team needs if it is to reach the top level. Big, strong and fast, he has become, at the age of 26, one of the best back-row tacklers of his day. He is yet another former stalwart of the world champion under-21 team that Jake White drew on to create the backbone of his future world title-holders. Smith was also recruited by Rudolf Straeuli to occupy the No.8 position and, at the age of 22, he played four matches in the Rugby World Cup 2003. He is a courageous captain for the Bloemfontein Cheetahs, but his ultimate dream in life is to lead the peaceful life of a farmer – earning him the nickname of the 'quiet killer of Springbok rugby'.

For once, Bryan Habana (left) is behind the camera, as he captures for prosperity the gold medals of his colleagues Os Du Randt, John Smit and Jannie Du Plessis (left to right), the front-row players whose work enabled him to put on such a dazzling display.

Schalk **Burger**

FLANKER

Born 13/04/1983

6ft 5in, 17st 4lb

Franchise 2007:
Stormers

39 apps, 10 tries

RWC 2007:

5 matches, 2 tries

Nicknamed 'Hulk' on account of his devastating tackles, Burger was launched on his international career at the age of 20 by Rudolf Straeuli for the Rugby World Cup 2003, although he came on only three times as a substitute in Australia – long enough to score his first try on his debut against Georgia. A severe cervical injury resulted in an operation in the summer of 2006, from which he emerged with a titanium plate in the nape of his neck. Defying all the prognostics, he was back on the rugby pitch six months later. Although he did not score any tries during the Rugby World Cup 2007, he was at the heart of every battle, allowing his natural aggressiveness to speak for itself – an approach that led to a two-match suspension (against England and Tonga) after a dangerous tackle on the Samoan scrum-half Junior Poluleuligaga.

Bakkies **Botha**

LOCK

Born 22/09/1979

6ft 8in, 18st 8lb

Franchise 2007: Bulls

44 apps, 7 tries

RWC 2007:

7 matches

Since coinciding with Victor Matfield in the Pretoria Bulls in 2001, Bakkies Botha has become his inseparable accomplice, the bull terrier who cleans up around the Springbok albatross. Botha and his 'brother' now constitute a peerless second row that has lived through the disastrous 2003 campaign in Australia (elimination in quarter-finals) and, above all, the seven glorious matches of the 2007 tournament. Botha, whose first name is derived from the shape of his bowed legs ('bakked' in slang), had acquired a reputation for hot-headedness that exasperated his coaches. His extended absence in 2006 seems to have left him with a much-needed sense of moderation.

Victor **Matfield**

LOCK

Born 11/05/1977

6ft 7in, 17st 4lb

Club 2007–08:
Toulon (D2, FRA)

67 apps, 5 tries

RWC 2007:

7 matches

The 30-year-old lock, until recently a member of the Pretoria Bulls, was acting captain three times in the summer of 2007, in place of an injured John Smit, and he was the vice-captain of Jake White's team, as well as being one of its key elements. His exceptional physique (6 ft 7 in, 17 stone 4 lb), his soaring jumps, his speed and his meticulous video analyses made him the tournament's king of the lineout. In 2007, he entered the history of Springbok rugby on two fronts, as he was also the captain of the first South African club to win the Super 14. He has decided 'to ensure the financial future of [his] family' by signing up with Toulon in the French Pro D2 for the 2007–08 season, along with George Gregan.

CJ **Van der Linde**

PROP

Born 27/08/1980

6ft 3in, 19st 2lb

Franchise 2007:
Cheetahs

47 apps, 4 tries

RWC 2007:

6 matches, 1 try

A typical product of the famous Grey College in Bloemfontein, Van der Linde is equally at home playing as a loose-head or tight-head prop. He first played for the Springboks at the precocious age of 22, first at Murrayfield then at Twickenham, in November 2002. After sitting out ten tests on the substitutes' bench, the Cheetahs' right prop finally established himself as the Springbok No.3 in the winter of 2004. Less acclaimed than the captain John Smit or the returning Du Randt, he nevertheless had an excellent Rugby World Cup. Fast for his size (6 ft 3 in, 19 stone 2 lb), Christoffel Johannes Van der Linde is also a dextrous handler of the ball. Although extremely unsettled by the Argentinean Rodrigo Roncero in the semi-finals, he contributed wholeheartedly to both the tackling and scrummages of the final.

Os **Du Randt**

Os is a beam (6 ft 3 in, 19 stone 9 lb) and around this beam, Jake White built his world champion pack. Jacobus Du Randt owes his nickname – 'Os' means 'buffalo' in Afrikaans – to his phenomenal strength. A prop for the world champion team in 1995, Du Randt retreated from the international scene after the 1999 World Rugby Cup (when the Springboks finished third) to his farm in Theunissen, 30 miles from Bloemfontein. This is where White went to seek him out in June 2004. A light 2007 (four matches in the Super 14 and two complete tests for South Africa) allowed the old buffalo to reach top form for the French campaign and join the Australians Jason Little, Tim Horan and John Eales (winners in 1991 and 1999) in the extremely select club of players that have been world champions on two occasions.

PROP

Born 08/09/1972

6ft 3in, 19st 9lb

Franchise 2007: Cheetahs

80 apps, 5 tries

RWC 2007:

6 matches

Bismarck **Du Plessis**

As a substitute for John Smit in both the Natal Sharks and the Springboks, Bismarck Du Plessis took advantage of the South African captain's absence to enjoy a superb season in the Super 14 of 2006. This earned him a call from White for the undervalued final of the 2007 Tri Nations (he was the first-choice hooker for the 6–33 defeat against the All Blacks in Christchurch) and for the squad of 30 for the Rugby World Cup in France. Du Plessis sat on the substitutes' bench five times, but he did go on to the pitch for four minutes in the semi-final then, as a temporary replacement for Smit, for five minutes against England in the final.

135

HOOKER

Born 22/05/1984

6ft 2in, 16st 7lb

Franchise 2007: Sharks

10 apps, 1 try

RWC 2007:

5 matches

Wikus **Van Heerden**

The wing forward for the Bulls was out of luck: he was removed from his post by the monumental Schalk Burger. The 'Hulk's' suspension did enable him, however, to start the matches against both Tonga and the United States (he was one of the few Springboks to remain unruffled in the former match). In the late summer of 2003, Rudolf Straeuli excluded the son of the Springbok lock Moaner Van Heerden from the squad for the Rugby World Cup in Australia. He had to wait for four years to be recalled to the Springboks, in July 2007 ... for two low-key matches, as White had decided to send a B team to compete in the last two tests of the Tri Nations, in Australia and New Zealand, respectively.

FLANKER

Born 25/02/1979

6ft 5in, 16st 5lb

Franchise 2007: Lions

14 apps, 1 try

RWC 2007:

6 matches

Jannie **Du Plessis**

At the age of 24, Jannie Du Plessis was one of the young forwards sent by Jake White to get a taste of the Australian and New Zealander packs in the latter stages of the 2007 Tri Nations. White recalled his commitment and defensive skills in the course of the Rugby World Cup in France when B.J. Botha suffered a knee injury against the United States. Du Plessis, who plays for the Bloemfontein Cheetahs, subsequently benefited from another afflicted knee, this time that of Van der Linde, to start the quarter-final match against Fiji. The return of the Cheetahs' right prop sent Du Plessis back to the bench, leaving it only for the last five minutes of the semi-final against Argentina, to replace the exhausted old buffalo Os Du Randt.

PROP

Born 16/11/1982

6ft 2in, 18st 10lb

Franchise 2007: Cheetahs

4 apps.

RWC 2007:

2 matches

FULL-BACK

Born 10/03/1984

6ft 1in, 13st 5lb

Franchise 2007: Sharks

18 apps, 3 tries

Ruan **Pienaar**

Ruan Pienaar – no relation to François Pienaar, the captain of the 1995 world champions – was, along with Schalk Burger and Wikus Van Heerden, one of the three sons of former Springboks in Jake White's squad. His father, Gysie Pienaar, was the team's full-back in the early 1980s. Equally comfortable in the positions of scrum-half and fly-half, Ruan has inherited from his father expert kicking skills and a love of running. At the age of 22 , he was also part of the young group that White sent to finish off the barely contested 2007 Tri Nations. As a first-choice full-back against Tonga, he took the opportunity to score two tries, albeit without challenging the positions of the untouchable Percy Montgomery and Fourie Du Preez.

RWC 2007: 4 matches, 2 tries

FLANKER / NO.8

Born 03/07/1976

6ft 5in, 16st 7lb

Franchise 2007: Sharks

42 apps, 11 tries

Bob **Skinstad**

A car accident in 1999, a knee injury in 2000, a fractured arm and shoulder operation in 2002: Bob Skinstad's career has been dotted with misfortunes. As captain of the Springboks from June 2001 to June 2002, he missed out on the Rugby World Cup 2003, through injury. Feeling shunned, he left to join Newport in Wales in 2004, before a spell in a lower division in a London suburb. After being recruited by the Natal Sharks in 2007, he participated in the splendid run of John Smit's team (Super 14 finalist) and returned to the Springboks, at the age of 31. Skinstad played as captain and No.8 against Tonga, and was put on for the last five minutes of the semi-final against Argentina to bring an international career that began in 1997 to a dignified close.

RWC 2007: 4 matches, 1 try

PROP

Born 12/06/1981

6ft 2in, 19st 7lb

Franchise 2007: Lions

13 apps, 1 try

Gurthro **Steenkamp**

Jake White considers the 26-year-old left prop from the Pretoria Bulls the natural successor to Os Du Randt. Steenkamp was an international in all the junior categories and made his debut for the Springboks in the 2005 Tri Nations, participating in the double victory over the Wallabies. A serious injury then kept him out of the national side for almost two years. Steenkamp returned to the team in the spring of 2007 – while White was nurturing the old warhorse Os Du Randt – only to succumb to injury yet again in the Tri Nations, against Australia. He started the match against Tonga in the pool stage but was outplayed by the prop Kisi Pulu. He redeemed his reputation, however, by taking part in the last half-hour of the Springboks' superb performance against Fiji, after replacing … Os Du Randt.

RWC 2007: 2 matches

COACH

Born 13/12/1963

Appointed 2004

52 matches, 34 wins,

1 draw, 17 losses

Jake **White**

Once an atypical prop, Jake White (aged 43) was a precocious coach. Ever since the age of 19, he has made training rugby teams his life's work. He had coached at all levels from school to university, including the RAU in Johannesburg, prior to taking over the under-21 squad, which he led to the world crown in 2002. He took charge of the Springboks in June 2004 and drew on the rising talents of a new generation, as well as luring both Percy Montgomery and Os Du Randt out of their international retirement. With the help of the Australian Eddie Jones, he added attacking flair to the traditional South African power play. Above all, he succeeded in protecting his squad from the fierce criticism of commentators who considered that it was woefully lacking in non-white players.

After leading a South African team to the under-21 world title in 2002, Jake White achieved similar success with the 'big boys'. He was named best trainer of 2007.

Butch James, one of the least known of the 2007 Springboks, eludes a challenge from Jason Robinson. James would become a world champion, just as the tremendous English full-back had been before him.

ALSO:

B.J. Botha (prop, Sharks, 4 matches in the RWC 2007), **Gary Botha** (hooker, Bulls, 1 match), **Jean De Villiers** (centre, Stormers, 1 match), **Ricky Januarie** (fly-half, Lions, 2 matches), **Wayne Julies** (centre, Bulls, 1 match), **Johannes Muller** (lock, Sharks, 4 matches), **Akona Ndungane** (winger, Bulls, 1 match), **Wynand Olivier** (centre, Bulls, 3 matches), **Andre Pretorius** (scrum-half, Lions, 5 matches, 2 pts [1 C]), **Albert Van den Berg** (lock, Sharks, 2 matches), **Ashwin Willemse** (winger, Lions, 1 match).

Statis

tics

match by match

Sébastien Chabal is thwarted by the Argentinean defence.

Argentina – France:
17–12

SAINT-DENIS, Stade de France
Attendance: 79,312
Referee: Tony Spreadbury (ENG)

Argentina

15 I. Corleto
14 L. Borges
13 M. Contepomi
    (H. Senillosa, 48'–50' then permanently, 73')
12 F. Contepomi
11 H. Agulla
10 J. M. Hernández
9   A. Pichot (cap.)
8   L. Ostiglia (M. Durand, 73')
7   J. M. Leguizamon
6   J. M. Fernández Lobbe
5   P. Albacete
4   I. Fernández Lobbe
    (R. Alvarez-Kairelis, 28')
3   M. Scelzo (S. Gonzalez Bonorino, 64')
2   M. Ledesma
1   R. Roncero
1 Try: Corleto (28')
4 Penalties: F. Contepomi (5', 9', 24', 34')

France

15 C. Heymans
14 A. Rougerie
13 D. Traille (F. Michalak, 16'-24')
12 Y. Jauzion
11 C. Dominici
10 D. Skrela (F. Michalak, 62')
9   P. Mignoni (J.-B. Élissalde, 73')
8   R. Martin (J. Bonnaire, 60')
7   I. Harinordoquy
6   S. Betsen
5   J. Thion
4   F. Pelous (S. Chabal, 60')
3   P. De Villiers
2   R. Ibañez (cap.) (D. Szarzewski, 60')
1   O. Milloud

4 Penalties: Skrela (7', 31', 40', 60)

139

Match 2
SATURDAY 8 SEPTEMBER
POOL C

The All Blacks make a dramatic entrance.

New Zealand – Italy:
76–14
MARSEILLE, Stade Vélodrome
Attendance: 58,000
Referee: Wayne Barnes (ENG)

New Zealand

15	L. MacDonald
14	D. Howlett
13	M. Muliana (I. Toeava, 51')
12	L. McAlister
11	S. Sivivatu
10	D. Carter (A. Mauger, 61')
9	B. Kelleher (B. Leonard, 51')
8	R. So'oialo
7	R. McCaw (cap.) (C. Masoe, 61')
6	J. Collins (N. Tialata, 45'-55')
5	A. Williams (S. Lauaki, 71')
4	C. Jack
3	C. Hayman
2	K. Mealamu (A. Oliver, 51')
1	T. Woodcock (N. Tialata, 64')

11 Tries: McCaw (1', 5'), Howlett (12', 56', 58'), Muliana (15'), Sivivatu (17', 28'), Jack (50'), Collins (67', 69')
9 Conversions: Carter (1', 5', 13', 15', 18', 50', 57'), McAlister (68', 70')
1 Penalty: Carter (10')
1 Yellow Card: Hayman (42')

Italy

15	D. Bortolussi (E. Galon, 66')
14	K. Robertson
13	A. Masi
12	Mi. Bergamasco
11	M. Stanojevic
10	R. De Marigny
9	A. Troncon (P. Griffen, 66')
8	Ma. Bergamasco
7	S. Parisse
6	A. Zanni (R. Vosawai, 40')
5	M. Bortolami (cap.)
4	S. Dellape (V. Bernabo, 58')
3	L. Castrogiovanni
2	F. Ongaro (C. Festuccia, 57')
1	S. Perugini (A. Lo Cicero, 40')

2 Tries: Stanojevic (37'), Mi. Bergamasco (71')
2 Conversions : Bortolussi (38'), De Marigny (71')
1 Yellow Card: Perugini (61')

Match 3
SATURDAY 8 SEPTEMBER
POOL B

George Gregan in full flight leading the Wallabies.

Australia – Japan:
91–3
LYON, Stade Gerland
Attendance: 40,043
Referee: Alan Lewis (IRE)

Australia

15	C. Latham
14	A. Ashley-Cooper (D. Mitchell, 57')
13	S. Mortlock (cap.) (M. Gerrard, 68')
12	M. Giteau
11	L. Tuqiri
10	S. Larkham (B. Barnes, 54')
9	G. Gregan
8	G. Smith
7	W. Palu (S. Hoiles, 67')
6	R. Elsom
5	D. Vickerman
4	N. Sharpe (H. McMeniman, 50')
3	A. Baxter (G. Shepherdson, 50')
2	S. Moore (A. Freier, 68')
1	M. Dunning

13 Tries: Sharpe (18'), Elsom (22', 30', 41'), Ashley-Cooper (45'), Latham (52', 71'), Barnes (56', 75'), Mitchell (59', 65'), Smith (61'), Freier (80')
10 Conversions: Mortlock (24', 42', 45', 53', 56', 59', 65'), Giteau (72', 76', 80')
2 Penalties: Mortlock (9', 15')

Japan

15	T. Kusumi
14	T. Kitagawa
13	K. Taira
12	N. Oto
11	H. Onozawa
10	K. Ono
9	Y. Yatomi
8	T. Sasaki (cap.) (H. Makiri, 47')
7	H. Kiso
6	Y. Watanabe (H. Makiri, 8'-13')
5	L. Vatuvei
4	T. Kumagae
3	R. Yamamura
2	T. Inokuchi
1	M. Yamamoto

1 Penalty: Ono (37')

Match 4
SATURDAY 8 SEPTEMBER
POOL A

Mark Cueto of England is stopped by the United States winger Salesi Sika.

England – United States:
28–10
LENS, Stade Félix-Bollaert
Attendance: 36,755
Referee: Jonathan Kaplan (RSA)

England

15	M. Cueto
14	J. Lewsey
13	J. Noon
12	M. Catt (A. Farrell, 62')
11	J. Robinson (M. Tait, 65')
10	O. Barkley
9	S. Perry (P. Richards, 59')
8	T. Rees
7	L. Dallaglio
6	J. Worsley (L. Moody, 68')
5	B. Kay
4	S. Shaw (M. Corry, 62')
3	P. Vickery (cap.) (M. Stevens, 62')
2	M. Regan (G. Chuter, 62')
1	A. Sheridan

3 Tries: Robinson (34'), Barkley (40'), Rees (47')
2 Conversions: Barkley (40', 48')
3 Penalties: Barkley (6', 21', 30')
1 Yellow Card: Dallaglio (73')

United States

15	C. Wyles
14	S. Sika (V. Malifa, 51')
13	P. Emerick
12	V. Esikia
11	T. Ngwenya (A. Tuipolotu, 67')
10	M. Hercus (cap.)
9	C. Erskine
8	T. Clever
7	H. Bloomfield (I. Basauri, 55')
6	L. Stanfill
5	M. Mangan (H. Mexted, 68')
4	A. Parker
3	C. Osentowski
2	O. Lentz (B. Burdette, 51')
1	M. McDonald (M. Moekiola, 59')

1 Try: Moekiola (74')
1 Conversion: Hercus (75ᵉ)
1 Penalty: Hercus (8')
2 Yellow Cards: Esikia (29'), Emerick (80')

Match 5
SUNDAY 9 SEPTEMBER
POOL B

Shane Williams scored twice for Wales, who were shaken by the Canadians.

Wales – Canada:
42–17
NANTES, Stade de la Beaujoire
Attendance: 36,939
Referess: Alain Rolland (IRE)

Wales

15	K. Morgan (G. Thomas, 47')
14	M. Jones
13	T. Shanklin
12	S. Parker
11	S. Williams
10	J. Hook (S. Jones, 47')
9	D. Peel (cap.) (M. Phillips, 65')
8	M. Williams (C. Charvis, 38'-40' then permanently, 59')
7	A. Popham
6	J. Thomas
5	A. W. Jones
4	I. Gough
3	A. Jones (D. Jones, 69')
2	M. Rees (R. Thomas, 69')
1	G. Jenkins

5 Tries: Parker (51'), A.W. Jones (57'), S. Williams (60', 62'), Charvis (67')
4 Conversions: S. Jones (52', 58', 63', 68')
3 Penalties: Hook (9', 14', 21')

Canada

15	M. Pyke
14	D. Van der Merwe
13	C. Culpan
12	D. Spicer
11	J. Pritchard
10	A. Monro (R. Smith, 63')
9	M. Williams (cap.) (E. Fairhurst, 76')
8	D. Biddle (C. Yukes, 66')
7	S. M. Stephen
6	J. Cudmore (A. Carpenter, 60')
5	M. James
4	L. Tait (M. Burak, 68')
3	J. Thiel (M. Pletch, 33')
2	P. Riordan
1	R. Snow (D. Pletch, 56')

3 Tries: Cudmore (24'), Culpan (36'), Williams (44')
1 Conversion: Pritchard (36')

Match 6
SUNDAY 9 SEPTEMBER
POOL **A**

Schalk Burger passes the ball, watched by Semo Sititi.

South Africa – Samoa:
59–7

PARIS, Parc des Princes
Attendance: 44,859
Referee: Paul Honiss (NZL)

South Africa

15	P. Montgomery
14	J.-P. Pietersen
13	J. Fourie
12	J. De Villiers (F. Steyn, 43')
11	B. Habana
10	B. James (A. Pretorius, 58')
9	F. Du Preez (R. Januarie, 65')
8	J. Smith
7	D. Rossouw (W. Van Heerden, 65')
6	S. Burger
5	V. Matfield
4	Ba. Botha (J. Muller, 67')
3	C.J. Van der Linde
2	J. Smit (cap.) (B. Du Plessis, 64')
1	O. Du Randt (B.J. Botha, 51')

8 Tries: Habana (32', 56', 66', 76'), Montgomery (40', 52'), Fourie (46'), Pietersen (80')
5 Conversions: Montgomery (40', 46', 56', 66', 80')
3 Penalties: Montgomery (3', 10', 15')

Samoa

15	D. Lemi
14	L. Fa'atau
13	G. Williams
12	J. Meafou (B. Lima, 60'; then T. Fuga, 65')
11	A. Tuilagi
10	E. Fuimano Sapolu (L. Crichton, 57')
9	J. Poluleuligaga
8	S. Sititi (cap.)
7	H. Tuilagi (A. Vaeluaga, 57')
6	D. Leo
5	K. Thompson
4	I. Tekori (J. Purdie, 55')
3	C. Johnston
2	M. Schwalger
1	J. Va'a (K. Lealamanu'a, 62')

1 Try: Williams (17')
1 Conversion: Williams (18')

Match 7
SUNDAY 9 SEPTEMBER
POOL **C**

Ross Ford gets the better of the heroic Portuguese defence.

Scotland – Portugal:
56–10

ST-ÉTIENNE, Stade Geoffroy-Guichard
Attendance: 34,162
Referee: Steve Walsh (NZL)

Scotland

15	R. Lamont
14	S. Lamont
13	M. Di Rollo (H. Southwell, 52')
12	R. Dewey
11	S. Webster
10	D. Parks (C. Paterson, 58')
9	M. Blair (R. Lawson, 65')
8	A. Hogg
7	S. Taylor
6	J. White (cap.) (K. Brown, 62')
5	S. Murray (S. MacLeod, 62')
4	N. Hines
3	E. Murray
2	S. Lawson (R. Ford, 70')
1	A. Jacobsen (G. Kerr, 36')

8 Tries: R. Lamont (12', 14'), S. Lawson (23'), Dewey (30'), Parks (57'), Southwell (59'), Brown (68'), Ford (75')
8 Conversions: Parks (12', 14', 23', 30', 57'), Paterson (59', 68', 75')

Portugal

15	P. Leal
14	Da. Mateus
13	F. Sousa (M. Portela de Morais, 38')
12	Di. Mateus
11	P. Carvalho
10	D. Cardoso Pinto
9	J. Pinto (P. Cabral, 64'; then L. Pissarra, 65')
8	V. Uva (cap.)
7	J. Uva (D. Coutinho, 64')
6	J. Severino Somoza
5	D. Penalva (P. Murinello, 52')
4	G. Uva
3	C. Spachuck
2	J. Ferreira (J. Correia, 52')
1	R. Cordeiro (J. Murre, 59')

1 Try: Carvalho (28')
1 Conversion: Cardoso Pinto (28')
1 Yellow Card: J. Uva (40')

Match 8
SUNDAY 9 SEPTEMBER
POOL **D**

The Namibian Tertius Losper makes life difficult for the Irish team.

Ireland – Namibia:
32–17

BORDEAUX, Stade J.-Chaban-Delmas
Attendance: 31,000
Referee: Joël Jutge (FRA)

Ireland

15	G. Dempsey
14	A. Trimble
13	B. O'Driscoll (cap.) (G. Murphy, 80')
12	G. D'Arcy
11	D. Hickie
10	R. O'Gara (P. Wallace, 80')
9	P. Stringer
8	D. Wallace (N. Best, 69')
7	D. Leamy
6	S. Easterby
5	P. O'Connell
4	D. O'Callaghan
3	J. Hayes
2	R. Best (J. Flannery, 62')
1	M. Horan (S. Best, 62')

5 Tries: O'Driscoll (4'), Trimble (19'), Easterby (30'), Penalty try (46'), Flannery (75')
2 Conversions: O'Gara (5', 49')
1 Penalty: O'Gara (17')

Namibia

15	T. Losper
14	R. Witbooi (M. Africa, 80')
13	B. Langenhoven
12	P. Van Zyl
11	H. Bock
10	É. Wessels
9	E. Jantjies (J. Van Tonder, 51')
8	H. Senekal (M. McKenzie, 22')
7	J. Burger
6	J. Nieuwenhuis
5	N. Esterhuyse
4	W. Kazombiaze
3	J. Du Toit
2	H. Horn (J. M. Meyer, 77')
1	K. Lensing (cap.)

2 Tries: Nieuwenhuis (60'), Van Zyl (63')
2 Conversions: Wessels (60', 64')
1 Penalty: Wessels (40')

Match 9
TUESDAY 11 SEPTEMBER
POOL **D**

Georgia posed a threat throughout the first half.

Argentina – Georgia:
33–3

LYON, Stade Gerland
Attendance: 40,240
Referee: Nigel Owens (SCO)

Argentina

15	I. Corleto
14	L. Borges (H. Senillosa, 69')
13	G. Tiesi
12	F. Contepomi (cap.) (F. Todeschini, 74')
11	F. Martin Aramburu
10	J. M. Hernández
9	N. Fernandez Miranda
8	J. M. Leguizamon (M. Schusterman, 61')
7	J. M. Fernández Lobbe
6	M. Durand
5	P. Albacete
4	R. Alvarez-Kairelis (E. Lozada, 68')
3	S. Gonzalez Bonorino (O. Hasan, 45')
2	M. Ledesma (A. Vernet Basualdo, 68')
1	M. Ayerza

4 Tries: Borges (47', 56'), Albacete (72'), Martin Aramburu (80')
2 Conversions: F. Contepomi (47'), Hernández (80')
3 Penalties: F. Contepomi (12', 35', 54')

Georgia

15	P. Jimsheladze (G. Shnikin, 59')
14	I. Machkhaneli
13	M. Urjukashvili (R. Gigauri, 74')
12	I. Giorgadze
11	B. Khamashuridze
10	M.-M. Kvirikashvili
9	I. Abuseridze (B. Samkharadze, 64')
8	B. Udesiani (V. Didebulidze, 65')
7	G. Labadze
6	G. Chkhaidze (Z. Maisuradze, 50')
5	M. Gorgodze
4	I. Zegdinidze (cap.)
3	D. Zirakashvili (A. Kopaliani, 41')
2	A. Giorgadze
1	D. Khinchagishvili (G. Shvelidze, 63')

1 Penalty: Kvirikashvili (3')

Match 10
WEDNESDAY 12 SEPTEMBER
POOL A

Tonga's captain Pierre Hola leads a charge.

Tonga – United States:
25–15

MONTPELLIER, Stade de la Mosson
Attendance: 24,243
Referee: Stuart Dickinson (AUS)

Tonga

15 V. Lilo
14 T. Tu'ifua
13 S. Hufanga
12 E. Taione (I. Tupou, 71')
11 J. Vaka (A. Havili, 61')
10 P. Hola
9 S. Havea (S. Tu'ipulotu, 41')
8 P. Latu (cap.) (V. Vaki, 65')
7 F. Maka (O. Filipine, 65')
6 H. T-Pole
5 K. Hehea
4 L. Fa'aoso
3 K. Pulu
2 A. Lutui (E. Taukafa, 76')
1 S. Tonga'uiha (T. Toke, 66')

3 Tries: Maka (2'), Vaka (57'), Vaki (70')
2 Conversions: Hola (3', 70')
2 Penalties: Hola (13', 26')

United States

15 C. Wyles
14 S. Sika
13 A. Tuipolotu
12 V. Esikia (P. Eloff, 61')
11 T. Ngwenya
10 M. Hercus (cap.)
9 C. Erskine
8 T. Clever
7 H. Bloomfield (I. Basauri, 54')
6 L. Stanfill
5 M. Mangan
4 A. Parker
3 C. Osentowski
2 O. Lentz (B. Burdette, 49')
1 M. McDonald (M. Moekiola, 54')

2 Tries: McDonald (48'), Stanfill (66')
1 Conversion: Hercus (66')
1 Penalty: Hercus (32')

Match 11
WEDNESDAY 12 SEPTEMBER
POOL B

Japan bravely resisted the Fijians before losing by just four points.

Fiji – Japan:
35–31

TOULOUSE, Stade Municipal
Attendance: 34,995
Referee: Marius Jonker (RSA)

Fiji

15 K. Ratuvou
14 V. Delasau (N. Ligairi, 70')
13 S. Rabeni
12 S. Baï
11 I. Neiuva
10 N. Little
9 M. Rauluni
8 S. Koyamaibole (N. Talei, 68')
7 A. Qera (A. Ratuva, 58')
6 S. Naevo
5 W. Lewaravu
4 K. Leawere
3 H. Qiodravu (J. Railomo, 68')
2 S. Koto
1 G. Dewes

4 Tries: Qera (36', 49'), Rabeni (57'), Leawere (71')
3 Conversions: Little (36', 49', 71')
3 Penalties: Little (3', 55', 74')
1 Yellow Card: Delasau (40')

Japan

15 G. Aruga (H. Onozawa, 60')
14 C. Loamanu
13 Y. Imamura
12 S. Onishi
11 K. Endo
10 B. Robins
9 T. Yoshida (Y. Yatomi, 59', and K. Taira, 65')
8 T. Miuchi (cap.)
7 P. O'Reilly
6 H. Makiri
5 L. Thompson
4 H. Ono
3 T. Soma (R. Yamamura, 68ᵉ)
2 Y. Matsubara
1 T. Nishiura

3 Tries: Thompson (51', 78'), Soma (61')
2 Conversions: Onishi (51', 78')
4 Penalties: Onishi (19', 29', 40', 42')

Match 12
WEDNESDAY 12 SEPTEMBER
POOL C

A clash of titans took place in Marseille.

Italy – Romania:
24–18

MARSEILLE, Stade Vélodrome
Attendance: 44,000
Referee: Tony Spreadbury (ENG)

Italy

15 D. Bortolussi (E. Galon, 49')
14 K. Robertson
13 G. Canale
12 Mi. Bergamasco
11 M. Stanojevic
10 R. Pez
9 P. Griffen (A. Troncon, 49')
8 Ma. Bergamasco
7 S. Parisse
6 J. Sole (R. Vosawai, 49')
5 M. Bortolami (cap.)
4 S. Dellape (V. Bernabo, 8')
3 L. Castrogiovanni
2 C. Festuccia
1 A. Lo Cicero

2 Tries: Dellape (6'), Penalty Try (53')
1 Conversion: Pez (53')
4 Penalties: Bortolussi (13'), Pez (62', 66', 72')

Romania

15 I. Dumitras (D. Vlad, 79')
14 C. Fercu
13 C. Gal
12 R. Gontineac
11 G. Brezoianu
10 I. Dimofte
9 L. Sirbu (V. Calafeteanu, 80')
8 A. Manta (M. Tudori, 80')
7 O. Tonita (C. Ratiu, 72')
6 F. Corodeanu
5 C. Petre
4 S. Socol
3 P. Balan
2 M. Tincu (R. Mavrodin, 70')
1 P. Toderasc (C. Popescu, 64')

2 Tries: Manta (42'), Tincu (47')
1 Conversion: Dimofte (46')
2 Penalties: Dimofte (70', 74')

Match 13
FRIDAY 14 SEPTEMBER
POOL A

Fourie Du Preez leaves Paul Sackey far behind.

South Africa – England:
36–0

SAINT-DENIS, Stade de France
Attendance: 79,000
Referee: Joël Jutge (FRA)

South Africa

15 P. Montgomery
14 J.-P. Pietersen
13 J. Fourie
12 F. Steyn (W. Olivier, 75')
11 B. Habana (R. Pienaar, 55'-59')
10 B. James (A. Pretorius, 70')
9 F. Du Preez (R. Pienaar, 66')
8 D. Rossouw
7 J. Smith (B. Skinstad, 70')
6 W. Van Heerden
5 V. Matfield
4 Ba. Botha (J. Muller, 52')
3 B.J. Botha
2 J. Smit (cap.) (B. Du Plessis, 70')
1 O. Du Randt (C.J. Van der Linde, 60')

3 Tries: Smith (5'), Pietersen (38', 62')
3 Conversions: Montgomery (6', 39', 63')
5 Penalties: Steyn (10'), Montgomery (36', 46', 54', 78')

England

15 J. Robinson (M. Tait, 57')
14 J. Lewsey
13 J. Noon (P. Richards, 79')
12 A. Farrell
11 P. Sackey
10 M. Catt
9 S. Perry (A. Gomarsall, 40')
8 N. Easter
7 T. Rees (L. Moody, 53')
6 M. Corry (cap.)
5 B. Kay
4 S. Shaw (S. Borthwick, 54'-58', then permanently, 78')
3 M. Stevens
2 M. Regan (G. Chuter, 55')
1 A. Sheridan (P. Freshwater, 78')

Match 14
SATURDAY 15 SEPTEMBER
POOL C

Isaia Toeava scores one of New Zealand's 16 tries.

New Zealand – Portugal:
108–13

LYON, Stade Gerland
Attendance: 40,729
Referee: Chris White (ENG)

New Zealand

15	M. Muliaina (L. MacDonald, 6ᵉ)
14	I. Toeava
13	C. Smith
12	A. Mauger
11	J. Rokocoko
10	N. Evans
9	B. Leonard (A. Ellis, 53′)
8	C. Masoe
7	S. Lauaki
6	J. Collins (cap.) (K. Mealamu, 63′)
5	A. Williams (R. So'oialo, 53′)
4	C. Jack (C. Hayman, 51′)
3	G. Somerville (T. Woodcock, 60′)
2	A. Hore (A. Oliver, 56′)
1	N. Tialata

16 Tries: Rokocoko (3′, 11′), Toeava (25′), Williams (27′), Mauger (29′, 65′), Collins (32′), Masoe (34′), Hore (40′), Leonard (50′), Evans (58′), Ellis (61′), MacDonald (69′), Smith (72′, 79′), Hayman (75′)
14 Conversions: Evans (12′, 26′, 28′, 30′, 32′, 40′, 50′, 58′, 61′, 65′, 69′, 72′, 75′, 79′)

Portugal

15	P. Leal
14	A. Aguilar
13	M. Portela de Morais
12	Di. Mateus
11	P. Carvalho
10	G. Malheiro (D. Cardoso Pinto, 40′)
9	L. Pissarra (J. Pinto, 40′)
8	D. Coutinho (T. Girao, 44′)
7	V. Uva (cap.) (J. Ferreira, 64′)
6	P. Murinello (J. Uva, 50′)
5	G. Uva
4	M. D'Orey (D. Penalva, 26′)
3	C. Spachuck
2	J. Correia
1	A. Silva (R. Cordeiro, 41′)

1 Try: Cordeiro (48′)
1 Conversion: Cardoso Pinto (48′)
1 Penalty : Cardoso Pinto (74′)
1 Drop Goal : Malheiro (22′)

Match 15
SATURDAY 15 SEPTEMBER
POOL B

Drew Mitchell was shown a yellow card but Australia still ran rampant.

Australia – Wales:
32–20

CARDIFF, Millennium Stadium
Attendance: 71,022
Referee: Steve Walsh (NZL)

Australia

15	C. Latham
14	D. Mitchell
13	S. Mortlock (cap.) (S. Staniforth, 41′)
12	M. Giteau
11	L. Tuqiri
10	B. Barnes (J. Huxley, 78′)
9	G. Gregan
8	W. Palu (S. Hoiles, 66′)
7	G. Smith (P. Waugh, 63′)
6	R. Elsom (M. Chisholm, 76′)
5	D. Vickerman
4	N. Sharpe
3	G. Shepherdson (A. Baxter, 72′)
2	S. Moore (A. Freier, 68′)
1	M. Dunning

4 Tries: Giteau (16′), Mortlock (35′), Latham (40′, 59′)
3 Conversions: Mortlock (16′, 40′), Giteau (60′)
1 Penalty: Mortlock (2′)
1 Drop Goal: Barnes (23′)
2 Yellow Cards: Mitchell (66′), Sharpe (75′)

Wales

15	G. Thomas (cap.) (J. Hook, 22′)
14	M. Jones
13	T. Shanklin
12	S. Parker (K. Morgan, 18′)
11	S. Williams
10	S. Jones
9	D. Peel (M. Phillips, 70′)
8	J. Thomas
7	M. Williams
6	C. Charvis (A. Popham, 12′-16′ then 48′-61′)
5	A. W. Jones
4	I. Gough (M. Owen, 65′)
3	Ad. Jones (D. Jones, 66′)
2	M. Rees (R. Thomas, 66′)
1	G. Jenkins

2 Tries: J. Thomas (45′), S. Williams (75′)
2 Conversions: Hook (46′, 76′)
2 Penalties: S. Jones (6′), Hook (53′)

Match 16
SATURDAY 15 SEPTEMBER
POOL D

The Georgians (in white) fall short against Ireland.

Ireland – Georgia:
14–10

BORDEAUX, Stade J.-Chaban-Delmas
Attendance: 33,807
Referee: Wayne Barnes (ENG)

Ireland

15	G. Dempsey
14	S. Horgan
13	B. O'Driscoll (cap.)
12	G. D'Arcy
11	D. Hickie
10	R. O'Gara
9	P. Stringer (I. Boss, 70′)
8	D. Leamy
7	D. Wallace
6	S. Easterby (N. Best, 72′)
5	P. O'Connell
4	D. O'Callaghan
3	J. Hayes (S. Best, 66′)
2	R. Best (J. Flannery, 52′)
1	M. Horan

2 Tries: R. Best (17′), Dempsey (55′)
2 Conversions: O'Gara (17′, 55′)
1 Yellow Card: Wallace (36′)

Georgia

15	O. Barkalaia (I. Machkhaneli, 34′)
14	G. Shkinin
13	M. Urjukashvili
12	D. Katcharava
11	G. Elizbarashvili (O. Eloshvili, 51′)
10	M. Kvirikashvili
9	B. Samkharadze (I. Abuseridze, 72′)
8	R. Urushadze
7	G. Chkhaidze
6	I. Maisuradze
5	M. Gorgodze
4	I. Zedginidze (cap.) (L. Datunashvili, 32′)
3	A. Kopaliani (D. Dhinchagishvili, 48′)
2.	G. Shvelidze
1.	M. Magrakvelidze (A. Giorgadze, 47′)

1 Try: Shkinin (45′)
1 Conversion: Kvirikashvili (45′)
1 Penalty: Kvirikashvili (37′)

Match 17
SUNDAY 16 SEPTEMBER
POOL B

Morgan Williams and the Canadians could not rise to the Fijian challenge.

Fiji – Canada:
29–16

CARDIFF, Millennium Stadium
Attendance: 21,175
Referee: Tony Spreadbury (ENG)

Fiji

15	K. Ratuvou
14	V. Delasau
13	S. Rabeni (M. Kunavore, 63′)
12	S. Baï
11	I. Neivua (N. Ligairi, 76′)
10	N. Little
9	M. Rauluni (cap.)
8	A. Qera
7	S. Koyamaibole
6	S. Naevo (N. Talei, 62′)
5	I. Rawaqa
4	K. Leawere
3	J. Railomo (H. Qiodravu, 62′)
2	S. Koto (V. Sauturaga, 70′)
1	G. Dewes

4 Tries : Leawere (21′), Ratuvou (27′, 80′), Delasau (42′)
3 Conversions: Little (27′, 42′, 80′)
1 Penalty: Little (7′)

Canada

15	M. Pyke
14	D. Van der Merwe
13	C. Culpan
12	D. Spicer
11	J. Pritchard
10	R. Smith
9	M. Williams (cap.)
8	D. Biddle (A. Carpenter, 68′)
7	S. Stephen (C. Yukes, 60′)
6	J. Cudmore
5	M. James
4	M. Burak (L. Tait, 65′)
3	J. Thiel
2	P. Riordan
1	R. Snow (D. Pletch, 62′)

1 Try: Smith (59′)
1 Conversion: Pritchard (60′)
3 Penalties: Pritchard (4′, 26′, 73′)

Match 18
SUNDAY 16 SEPTEMBER **POOL A**

The duel of Pacific nations narrowly went Tonga's way.

Tonga – Samoa:
19–15

MONTPELLIER, Stade de la Mosson
Attendance: 24,000
Referee: Jonathan Kaplan (RSA)

Tonga

15	V. Lilo
14	T. Tu'ifua (H. Tonga'uiha, 56')
13	S. Hufanga
12	E. Taione (I. Tupou, 73')
11	J. Vaka
10	P. Hola
9	E. Taufa (S. Tu'ipulotu, 43')
8	P. Latu (cap.)
7	F. Maka
6	H. T-Pole
5	K. Hehea
4	I. Afeaki
3	K. Pulu
2	E. Taukafa
1	S. Tonga'uiha (T. Toke, 73')

1 Try: Taione (60')
1 Conversion: Hola (60')
4 Penalties: Hola (2', 38' 47', 66')
2 Yellow Cards: Taione (27'), Toke (75')
1 Red Card: T-Pole (72')

Samoa

15	G. Williams (L. Lui, 80')
14	S. Tagicakibau (D. Lemi, 56')
13	E. Seveali'i
12	S. Mapusua
11	A. Tuilagi
10	L. Crichton
9	S. So'oialo
8	U. Ulia (J. Purdie, 62')
7	S. Sititi (cap.)
6	D. Leo
5	K. Thompson
4	I. Tekori (L. Lafaiali'i, 62')
3	C. Johnston (M. Salanoa, 56')
2	M. Schwalger (T. Fuga, 59')
1	J. Va'a

5 Penalties: Williams (5', 19', 24', 28', 69')

Match 19
SUNDAY 16 SEPTEMBER **POOL D**

Frédéric Michalak (centre) and the French regained their smiles.

France – Namibia:
87–10

TOULOUSE, Stade Municipal
Attendance: 35,000
Referee: Alain Rolland (IRE)

France

15	C. Poitrenaud (A. Rougerie, 66')
14	V. Clerc
13	D. Marty
12	D. Traille (Y. Jauzion, 51')
11	C. Heymans
10	F. Michalak (L. Beauxis, 63')
9	J.-B. Élissalde (cap.)
8	J. Bonnaire
7	T. Dusautoir
6	Y. Nyanga (I. Harinordoquy, 55')
5	L. Nallet
4	S. Chabal (F. Pelous, 58')
3	P. De Villiers (N. Mas, 41')
2	D. Szarzewski (R. Ibañez, 58')
1	J.-B. Poux

13 Tries: Heymans (7'), Marty (12'), Dusautoir (21'), Nallet (3', 40') Clerc (38', 59', 65'), Bonnaire (47'), Chabal (49', 54'), Élissalde (56'), Ibañez (75')
11 Conversions: Élissalde (12', 21', 32', 38', 40', 47', 49', 54', 56', 59', 65')

Namibia

15	T. Losper
14	R. Witbooi
13	B. Langenhoven
12	P. Van Zyl (M. Africa, 66e)
11	H. Bock
10	É. Wessels (L.-W. Botes, 12')
9	J. Van Tonder (E. Jantjies, 41')
8	M. McKenzie
7	J. Burger (T. Du Plessis, 57')
6	J. Nieuwenhuis
5	N. Esterhuyse (H. Lintvelt, 57')
4	W. Kazombiaze
3	J. Du Toit
2	H. Horn (J. M. Meyer, 65')
1	K. Lensing (cap.) (J. Redelinghuys, 57')

1 Try: Langenhoven (79')
1 Conversion: Losper (79')
1 Drop Goal: Wessels (10')
1 Red Card: Nieuwenhuis (19')

Match 20
TUESDAY 18 SEPTEMBER **POOL C**

Mike Blair was stopped short here, but Scotland still scored six tries.

Scotland – Romania:
42–0

EDINBURGH, Murrayfield
Attendance: 31,222
Referee: Nigel Owens (WAL)

Scotland

15	R. Lamont
14	S. Lamont
13	S. Webster
12	R. Dewey (H. Southwell, 59')
11	C. Paterson
10	D. Parks (N. Walker, 68')
9	M. Blair (C. Cusiter, 59')
8	S. Taylor
7	A. Hogg (K. Brown, 65')
6	J. White (cap.)
5	J. Hamilton
4	N. Hines (S. MacLeod, 52')
3	E. Murray
2	R. Ford (S. Lawson, 59')
1	G. Kerr (C. Smith, 52')

6 Tries: Paterson (2'), Hogg (17', 46', 53'), R. Lamont (38', 72')
6 Conversions: Paterson (2', 17', 38', 46', 53', 72')

Romania

15	I. Dumitras
14	C. Fercu
13	C. Gal
12	R. Gontineac (F. Vlaicu, 74')
11	G. Brezoianu
10	I. Dimofte (I. Tofan, 45')
9	L. Sirbu (V. Calafeteanu, 45')
8	O. Tonita
7	A. Manta (M. Tudori, 53')
6	F. Corodeanu (C. Ratiu, 61')
5	C. Petre
4	S. Socol (cap.)
3	P. Balan (S. Florea, 69')
2	M. Tincu (R. Mavrodin, 41')
1	P. Toderasc

Match 21
WEDNESDAY 19 SEPTEMBER **POOL C**

The Italian captain Marco Bortolami dominates the lineout.

Italy – Portugal:
31–5

PARIS, Parc des Princes
Attendance: 45,476
Referee: Marius Jonker (RSA)

Italy

15	D. Bortolussi
14	P. Canavosio
13	G. Canale
12	A. Masi
11	M. Pratichetti
10	R. De Marigny
9	A. Troncon (P. Griffen, 49')
8	Ma. Bergamasco
7	R. Vosawai (S. orlando, 58')
6	S. Parisse
5	M. Bortolami (cap.)
4	C. Del Fava
3	L. Castrogiovanni (S. Perugini, 63')
2	L. Ghiraldini
1	A. Lo Cicero

3 Tries: Masi (4', 77'), Ma. Bergamasco (72')
2 Conversions: Bortolussi (4', 77')
4 Penalties: Bortolussi (10', 29', 40', 63')
1 Yellow Card: Bortolami (8')

Portugal

15	P. Cabral
14	Da. Mateus (G. Foro, 61')
13	F. Sousa
12	Di. Mateus (D. Gama, 31')
11	A. Aguilar
10	D. Cardoso Pinto
9	J. Pinto (L. Pissarra, 66')
8	J. Uva (P. Murinello, 63')
7	V. Uva (cap.)
6	T. Girao
5	G. Uva
4	D. Penalva
3	C. Spachuck (A. Silva, 60')
2	J. Correia (D. Figueiredo, 69')
1	R. Cordeiro (J. Murre, 61')

1 Try: Penalva (33')

Match 22
THURSDAY 20 SEPTEMBER
POOL B

James Hook leads a forceful Welsh attack.

Wales – Japan:
72–18

CARDIFF, Millennium Stadium
Attendance: 42,558
Referee: Joël Jutge (FRA)

Wales

15 K. Morgan
14 D. James
13 J. Robinson (T. Shanklin, 73')
12 J. Hook
11 S. Williams
10 S. Jones (cap.) (C. Sweeney, 54')
9   M. Phillips (G. Cooper, 57')
8   C. Charvis
7   A. Popham (M. Owen, 58')
6   M. Williams
5   A. W. Jones (I. Evans, 52')
4   W. James
3   C. Horsman (G. Jenkins, 65')
2   R. Thomas (H. Bennett, 59')
1   D. Jones

11 Tries: A. W. Jones (11'), Hook (24'), R. Thomas (32'), Morgan (40' + 1), Phillips (42'), S. Williams (49', 80'), James (53'), Cooper (59'), M. Williams (64', 74')
7 Conversions: S. Jones (11', 24', 32', 40' + 1, 53'), Sweeney (64', 74')
1 Penalty: S. Jones (6')

Japan

15 C. Loamanu
14 K. Endo
13 Y. Imamura (K. Taira, 51')
12 S. Onishi (T. Kusumi, 52')
11 H. Onozawa
10 B. Robins
9   T. Yoshida (K. Chulwon, 66')
8   P. O'Reilly
7   T. Miuchi (cap.)
6   H. Makiri (Y. Watanabe, 52')
5   L. Thompson
4   H. Ono
3   T. Soma
2   Y. Matsubara (T. Inokuchi, 74')
1   T. Nishiura (R. Yamamura, 68')

2 Tries: Endo (19'), Onozawa (57')
1 Conversion: Robins (57')
2 Penalties: Onishi (4', 35')

Match 23
FRIDAY 21 SEPTEMBER
POOL D

The French squad show solidarity before the clash against the Irish.

France – Ireland:
25–3

SAINT-DENIS, Stade de France
Attendance: 80,267
Referee: Chris White (ENG)

France

15 C. Poitrenaud (A. Rougerie, 72')
14 V. Clerc
13 D. Marty (Y. Jauzion, 74')
12 D. Traille
11 C. Heymans
10 F. Michalak
9   J.-B. Élissalde (L. Beauxis, 74')
8   J. Bonnaire
7   T. Dusautoir
6   S. Betsen (Y. Nyanga, 63')
5   J. Thion
4   S. Chabal (L. Nallet, 46')
3   P. De Villiers
2   R. Ibañez (cap.) (D. Szarzewski, 57')
1   O. Milloud (J.-B. Poux, 74')

2 Tries: Clerc (60', 69')
5 Penalties: Élissalde (7', 18', 22', 40', 55')
1 Yellow Card: Traille (76')

Ireland

15 G. Dempsey
14 S. Horgan
13 B. O'Driscoll (cap.)
12 G. D'Arcy
11 A. Trimble
10 R. O'Gara
9   E. Reddan
8   D. Leamy
7   D. Wallace
6   S. Easterby (N. Best, 73')
5   P. O'Connell
4   D. O'Callaghan (M. O'Kelly, 72')
3   J. Hayes (S. Best, 74')
2   J. Flannery (F. Sheahan, 50'-55', then permanently, 78')
1   M. Horan

1 Drop Goal: O'Gara (37')
1 Yellow Card: O'Connell (64')

Match 24
SATURDAY 22 SEPTEMBER
POOL A

The Tongans inflict shock treatment on André Pretorius.

South Africa – Tonga:
30–25

LENS, Stade Félix-Bollaert
Attendance: 40,069
Referee: Wayne Barnes (ENG)

South Africa

15 R. Pienaar
14 A. Willemse (B. Habana, 47')
13 W. Olivier
12 W. Julies (F. Steyn, 47')
11 J.-P. Pietersen
10 A. Pretorius (P. Montgomery, 59')
9   R. Januarie
8   D. Rossouw (J. Smith, 25'-30', then permanently 50')
7   B. Skinstad (cap.)
6   W. Van Heerden
5   A. Van den Berg (V. Matfield, 47')
4   Ba. Botha
3   CJ Van der Linde
2   G. Botha (J. Smit, 47')
1   G. Steenkamp (BJ Botha, 47')

4 Tries: Pienaar (18', 65'), Smith (59'), Skinstad (64')
2 Conversions: Pretorius (18'), Montgomery (59')
2 Penalties: Steyn (53'), Montgomery (75')
2 Yellow Cards: Steyn (63'), Habana (69')

Tonga

15 V. Lilo
14 T. Tu'ifua
13 S. Hufanga
12 E. Taione (I. Tupou, 76')
11 J. Vaka (A. Havili, 73')
10 P. Hola
9   S. Tu'ipulotu (S. Havea, 67')
8   F. Maka
7   P. Latu (cap.) (O. Filipine, 65')
6   V. Vaki
5   E. Kauhenga (I. Afeaki, 51')
4   K. Hehea
3   K. Pulu
2   A. Lutui (E. Taukafa, 67')
1   S. Tonga'uiha

3 Tries: Pulu (44'), Hufanga (70'), Vaki (72')
2 Conversions: Hola (44', 70')
2 Penalties: Hola (9', 78')
1 Yellow Card: Vaka (63')

Match 25
SATURDAY 22 SEPTEMBER
POOL A

Paul Sackey foils Iosefa Tekori and the Samoans.

England – Samoa:
44–22

NANTES, Stade de la Beaujoire
Attendance: 37,022
Referee: Alan Lewis (IRE)

England

15 J. Lewsey
14 P. Sackey
13 M. Tait (D. Hipkiss, 72')
12 O. Barkley
11 M. Cueto
10 J. Wilkinson
9   A. Gomarsall
8   J. Worsley (L. Moody, 70')
7   N. Easter
6   M. Corry (cap.)
5   B. Kay
4   S. Shaw (S. Borthwick, 65')
3   M. Stevens
2   G. Chuter
1   A. Sheridan (P. Freshwater, 65')

4 Tries: Corry (2', 77'), Sackey (33', 80')
3 Conversions: Wilkinson (2', 33', 77')
4 Penalties: Wilkinson (15', 21', 45', 71')
2 Drop Goals: Wilkinson (6', 70')

Samoa

15 L. Crichton
14 D. Lemi
13 S. Mapusua (J. Meafou, 70')
12 B. Lima (L. Lui, 72')
11 A. Tuilagi
10 E. Fuimaono Sapolu
9   J. Poluleuligaga (S. So'oialo, 66')
8   H. Tuilagi (A. Vaeluaga, 70')
7   S. Sititi (cap.)
6   D. Leo
5   K. Thompson
4   I. Tekori (J. Purdie, 75')
3   C. Johnston
2   M. Schwalger
1   K. Lealamanu'a

1 Try: Poluleuligaga (47')
1 Conversion: Crichton (47')
5 Penalties: Crichton (9', 12', 38', 40', 42')

Match 26
SATURDAY 22 SEPTEMBER
POOL D

The efficient Pumas stormed to the top of Pool D with a rout of Namibia.

Argentina – Namibia:
63–3

MARSEILLE, Stade Vélodrome
Attendance: 55,000
Referee: Stuart Dickinson (AUS)

Argentina
15 I. Corleto (F. Serra Miras, 65')
14 H. Senillosa
13 G. Tiesi
12 M. Contepomi
11 H. Agulla
10 F. Contepomi (F. Todeschini, 59')
9 A. Pichot (cap.)
     (N. Fernandez Miranda, 56')
8 J. Leguizamon (G. Longo, 59')
7 J. M. Fernández Lobbe
6 L. Ostiglia
5 P. Albacete
4 I. Fernández Lobbe
     (R. Alvarez-Kairelis, 66')
3 O. Hasan
2 A. Vernet Basualdo
1 R. Roncero (M. Scelzo, 66')

9 Tries: Roncero (25'), Leguizamon (35', 52'), M. Contepomi (38'), F. Contepomi (45'), Tiesi (55'), Corleto (58'), Penalty Try (63'), Todeschini (71')
6 Conversions: F. Contepomi (25', 38', 45', 52'), Todeschini (63', 71')
2 Penalties: F. Contepomi (10', 20')

Namibia
15 H. Bock
14 D. Mouton (B. Langenhoven, 53')
13 D. Grobler (P. Van Zyl, 51')
12 C. Powell (cap.)
11 M. Africa
10 M. Scheuder (J. Van Tonder, 73')
9 E. Jantjies
8 T. Du Plessis
7 J. Burger
6 M. McKenzie (H. Lintvelt, 39')
5 N. Esterhuyse
4 W. Kazombiaze (H. Senekal, 60')
3 M. Visser (K. Lensing, 41')
2 J. M. Meyer (H. Horn, 41')
1 J. Redelinghuys

1 Penalty: Schreuder (7')

Match 27
SUNDAY 23 SEPTEMBER
POOL B

Matt Giteau scored two of the Wallabies' seven tries against Fiji.

Australia – Fiji:
55–12

MONTPELLIER, Stade de la Mosson
Attendance: 32,231
Referee: Nigel Owens (WAL)

Australia
15 C. Latham
14 D. Mitchell
13 A. Ashley-Cooper
12 M. Giteau
11 L. Tuqiri
10 B. Barnes (S. Staniforth, 63', and J. Huxley, 67')
9 G. Gregan (cap.) (S. Cordingley, 58')
8 P. Waugh
7 W. Palu (S. Hoiles, 66')
6 R. Elsom (H. McMeniman, 58')
5 D. Vickerman
4 M. Chisholm
3 G. Shepherdson
2 S. Moore (A. Freier, 58')
1 M. Dunning (G. Holmes, 58')

7 Tries: Giteau (17', 36'), Mitchell (31', 70', 79'), Ashley-Cooper (57'), Hoiles (74')
4 Cons: Giteau (17', 31', 57', 70')
3 Penalties: Giteau (28', 42', 50')
1 Drop Goal: Barnes (44')

Fiji
15 N. Ligairi
14 V. Delasau
13 M. Kunavore (Lovobalavu, 65ᵉ)
12 S. Baï (cap.)
11 I. Neivua
10 W. Luveniyali (S. Rabeni, 41ᵉ)
9 J. Daunivucu (M. Rauluni, 41ᵉ)
8 J. Qovu
7 A. Ratuva
6 N. Talei (S. Koyamaibole, 63ᵉ)
5 I. Rawaqa
4 I. Domolailai (W. Lewaravu, 41ᵉ)
3 H. Qiodravu
2 V. Sauturaga
1 A. Yalayalatabua (J. Railomo, 60ᵉ)

2 Tries: Neivua (40'), Ratuva (47')
1 Conversion: Baï (47')

Match 28
SUNDAY 23 SEPTEMBER
POOL C

A blow on the nose is not enough to stop New Zealand's Sitiveni Sivivatu.

New Zealand – Scotland:
40–0

EDINBURGH, Murrayfield
Attendance: 64,558
Referee: Marius Jonker (RSA)

New Zealand
15 L. MacDonald (N. Evans, 21')
14 D. Howlett
13 C. Smith (I. Toeava, 66')
12 L. McAlister
11 S. Sivivatu
10 D. Carter
9 B. Kelleher (B. Leonard, 59')
8 R. McCaw (cap.) (S. Lauaki, 61')
7 R. So'oialo
6 C. Masoe
5 A. Williams (C. Jack, 66')
4 R. Thorne
3 C. Hayman (N. Tialata, 66')
2 A. Oliver (A. Hore, 59')
1 T. Woodcock

6 Tries: McCaw (6'), Howlett (15', 74'), Kelleher (32'), Williams (62'), Carter (65')
2 Conversions: Carter (6', 65')
2 Penalties: Carter (25', 43')

Scotland
15 H. Southwell
14 N. Walker
13 M. Di Rollo
12 A. Henderson (R. Dewey, 69')
11 S. Webster
10 C. Paterson (D. Parks, 21')
9 C. Cusiter (R. Lawson, 59')
8 D. Callam
7 J. Barclay
6 K. Brown
5 S. Murray (cap.)
4 S. MacLeod (J. Hamilton, 69')
3 C. Smith (G. Kerr, 51'-66')
2 S. Lawson (F. Thomson, 58')
1 A. Dickinson (G. Kerr, 66')

Match 29
TUESDAY 25 SEPTEMBER
POOL B

Kosuke Endo scored one of Japan's two tries in the draw against Canada.

Canada – Japan:
12–12

BORDEAUX, Stade J.-Chaban-Delmas
Attendance: 33,810
Referee: Jonathan Kaplan (RSA)

Canada
15 M. Pyke
14 D. Van der Merwe
13 C. Culpan (J. Mensah-Coker, 72')
12 D. Spicer
11 J. Pritchard
10 R. Smith
9 M. Williams (cap.)
8 A. Carpenter (M. Webb, 56')
7 A. Kleeberger (J. Jackson, 79')
6 C. Yukes
5 M. James
4 M. Burak
3 J. Thiel (S. Franklin, 58')
2 P. Riordan (M. Pletch, 60')
1 R. Snow (D. Pletch, 45')

2 Tries: Riordan (47'), Van der Merwe (66')
1 Conversion: Pritchard (66')

Japan
15 G. Aruga
14 K. Endo (H. Onozawa, 60)
13 Y. Imamura (K. Taira, 52)
12 S. Onishi
11 C. Loamanu
10 B. Robins
9 T. Yoshida (K. Chulwon, 50)
8 T. Miuchi (cap.) (H. Kiso, 74)
7 P. O'Reilly
6 H. Makiri
5 L. Thompson
4 H. Ono (L. Vatuvei, 56)
3 T. Soma (R. Yamamura, 52)
2 Y. Matsubara
1 T. Nishiura

2 Tries: Endo (12), Taira (80 + 4)
1 Conversion: Onishi (80 + 4)

Match 30
TUESDAY 25 SEPTEMBER
POOL C

Iuliuan Dumitras and Romania struggled to overcome Portugal.

Romania – Portugal:
14–10

TOULOUSE, Stade Municipal
Attendance: 35,532
Referee: Paul Honiss (NZL)

Romania
15 I. Dumitras
14 C. Nicolae
13 I. Dimofte
12 R. Gontineac
11 C. Fercu
10 D. Dumbrava
9. V. Calafeteanu (L. Sirbu, 63')
8. F. Corodeanu
7. O. Tonita (cap.) (V. Ursache, 66')
6. M. Tudori (S. Socol, 40')
5. C. Petre
4. C. Ratiu
3. P. Balan
2. R. Mavrodin (M. Tincu, 40')
1. C. Popescu

2 Tries: Tincu (62'), Corodeanu (73')
2 Conversions: Calafeteanu (62'), Dumbrava (73')

Portugal
15 P. Leal
14 Da. Mateus
13 F. Sousa
12 Di. Mateus
11 M. Portela de Morais
10 D. Cardoso Pinto
9 J. Pinto (G. Malheiro, 65', and L. Pissarra, 75')
8 J. Uva (P. Murinello, 76')
7. T. Girao
6 D. Coutinho
5 D. Penalva (S. Pahla, 79')
4 G. Uva
3 C. Spachuck (J. Correia, 50')
2 J. Ferreira (cap.) (J. Murre, 70')
1 R. Cordeiro

1 Try: Ferreira (18')
1 Conversion: Cardoso Pinto (18')
1 Penalty: Malheiro (69')

Match 31
WEDNESDAY 26 SEPTEMBER
POOL D

The Georgian team worked hard to earn their first victory.

Georgia – Namibia:
30–0

LENS, Stade Félix-Bollaert
Attendance: 32,451
Referee: Steve Walsh (NZL)

Georgia
15 M. Urjukashvili (R. Gigauri, 69')
14 I. Machkhaneli
13 D. Katcharava
12 A. Giorgadze
11 G. Shkinin (B. Khamashuridze, 47')
10 M. Kvirikashvili
9 I. Abuseridze (cap.) (B. Samkharadze, 56')
8 R. Urushadze (B. Udesiani, 51')
7 G. Chkhaidze
6 G. Labadze
5 M. Gorgodze (V. Didebulidze, 19')
4 L. Datunashvili
3 D. Zirakashvili
2 I. Giorgadze
1 G. Shvelidze

3 Tries: A. Giorgadze (38'), Machkhaneli (70'), Katcharava (80'+1)
3 Conversions: Kvirikashvili (38', 70', 80'+1)
3 Penalties: Kvirikashvili (8', 26', 68')

Namibia
15 H. Bock (E. Jantjies, 72')
14 R. Witbooi
13 P. Van Zyl
12 C. Powell
11 B. Langenhoven
10 M. Schreuder (M. Africa, 60')
9 J. Van Tonder
8 J. Burger
7 T. Du Plessis (N. Esterhuyse, 42')
6 J. Nieuwenhuis
5 H. Senekal (D. Kamonga, 72')
4 W. Kazombiaze
3 M. Visser (J. Du Toit, 41' and J. Redelinghuys, 52')
2 H. Horn (J. M. Meyer, 69')
1 K. Lensing (cap.)

Match 32
WEDNESDAY 26 SEPTEMBER
POOL A

Loki Crichton scored ten points as Samoa finished on a high note.

Samoa – United States:
25–21

ST-ÉTIENNE, Stade Geoffroy-Guichard
Attendance: 34,124
Referee: Wayne Barnes (ENG)

Samoa
15 L. Crichton
14 L. Fa'atau (D. Lemi, 60')
13 S. Mapusua
12 E. Seveali'i
11 A. Tuilagi
10 E. Fuimaono Sapolu (L. Lui, 70')
9 J. Poluleuligaga (S. So'oialo, 70')
8 J. Purdie
7 A. Vaeluaga
6 S. Sititi (cap.)
5 K. Thompson (I. Tekori, 64')
4 L. Lafaiali'i
3 C. Johnston
2 M. Schwalger (S. Vaisola Sefo, 73')
1 Lelamanu'a (N. Leleimalefaga, 70')

3 Tries: Fa'atau (5'), A. Tuilagi (9'), Thompson (36')
2 Conversions: Crichton (9', 36')
2 Penalties: Crichton (31', 72')
1 Yellow Card: Vaisola Sefo (75')

United States
15 C. Wiles
14 S. Sika
13 P. Eloff
12 V. Esikia (A. Tuipolotu, 73')
11 N. Ngwenya
10 M. Hercus (cap.)
9 C. Erskine
8 T. Clever (B. Burdette, 45')
7 F. Mo'unga (M. Aylor, 64')
6 L. Stanfill
5 H. Mexted
4 A. Parker
3 C. Osentowski
2 O. Lentz
1 M. McDonald (M. Moekiola, 68')

2 Tries: Ngwenya (53'), Stanfill (79')
1 Conversion: Hercus (53')
3 Penalties: Hercus (31', 64', 71')
1 Yellow Card: Mo'unga (52')

Match 33
FRIDAY 28 SEPTEMBER
POOL A

Peter Richards has to exert himself to stop the Tongan Aisea Havili.

England – Tonga:
36–20

PARIS, Parc des Princes
Attendance: 45,085
Referee: Alain Rolland (IRE)

England
15 J. Lewsey
14 P. Sackey (D. Hipkiss, 68')
13 M. Tait
12 O. Barkley (A. Farrell, 51')
11 M. Cueto (P. Richards, 73')
10 J. Wilkinson
9 A. Gomarsall
8 N. Easter
7 L. Moody
6 M. Corry (cap.) (L. Dallaglio, 64')
5 B. Kay
4 S. Borthwick
3 M. Stevens (P. Vickery, 57')
2 G. Chuter (L. Mears, 68')
1 A. Sheridan

4 Tries: Sackey (20', 38'), Tait (57'), Farrell (66')
2 Conversions: Wilkinson (57', 66')
2 Penalties: Wilkinson (13', 35')
2 Drop Goals: Wilkinson (32', 72')

Tonga
15 V. Lilo
14 T. Tu'ifua
13 S. Hufanga (H. Tonga'uiha, 60')
12 E. Taione
11 J. Vaka (A. Havili, 67')
10 P. Hola
9 S. Tu'ipulotu (S. Havea, 69')
8 P. Latu (cap.)
7 F. Maka
6 H. T-Pole
5 L. Fa'aoso
4 V. Vaki
3 K. Pulu
2 A. Lutui (E. Taukafa, 66')
1 S. Tonga'uiha (T. Filise, 47'-49', then permanently, 55')

2 Tries: Hufanga (17'), T-Pole (80')
2 Conversions: Hola (17', 80')
2 Penalties: Hola (9', 55')

Match 34
SATURDAY 29 SEPTEMBER
POOL C

Another crushing victory for Richie McCaw and his All Blacks.

New Zealand – Romania:
85–8

TOULOUSE, Stade Municipal
Attendance: 35,608
Referee: Joël Jutge (FRA)

New Zealand

15	N. Evans
14	J. Rokocoko
13	I. Toeava
12	A. Mauger
11	S. Sivivatu (C. Smith, 60')
10	L. McAlister (D. Howlett, 54')
9	A. Ellis (B. Leonard, 59')
8	S. Lauaki
7	C. Masoe (R. McCaw, 54')
6	J. Collins (cap.)
5	K. Robinson (C. Jack, 54')
4	R. Thorne
3	G. Somerville
2	K. Mealamu (A. Hore, 61')
1	N. Tialata

13 Tries: Sivivatu (1', 24'), Masoe (9'), Rokocoko (14', 57', 65'), Evans (17'), Mauger (37'), Toeava (46', 80'), Hore (63'), Smith (74'), Howlett (79')
10 Conversions: McAlister (9', 14', 24', 46'), Evans (57', 63', 65', 74', 79', 80')

Romania

15	I. Dumitras (F. Vlaicu, 61')
14	S. Ciuntu
13	C. Gal
12	R. Gontineac (C. Dascalu, 69')
11	G. Brezoianu
10	I. Dimofte
9	L. Sirbu (V. Calafeteanu, 61')
8	O. Tonita
7	A. Manta (V. Ursache, 67')
6	F. Corodeanu (C. Ratiu, 48')
5	C. Petre
4	S. Socol (cap.)
3	S. Florea
2	M. Tincu (R. Mavrodin, 52')
1	I. Paulica

1 Try: Tincu (30')
1 Penalty: Dimofte (71')

Match 35
SATURDAY 29 SEPTEMBER
POOL B

Chris Latham touches down with the sixth Australian try against Canada.

Australia – Canada:
37–6

BORDEAUX, Stade J.-Chaban-Delmas
Attendance: 33,805
Referee: Chris White (ENG)

Australia

15	C. Latham
14	C. Shepherd
13	L. Tuqiri
12	A. Ashley-Cooper
11	D. Mitchell
10	J. Huxley
9	S. Cordingley (G. Gregan, 74')
8	D. Lyons (S. Hoiles, 46')
7	G. Smith (cap.)
6	H. McMeniman
5	M. Chisholm
4	N. Sharpe (P. Waugh, 71')
3	A. Baxter
2	A. Freier (S. Hardman, 61')
1	G. Holmes

6 Tries: Baxter (26'), Freier (34'), Smith (51'), Mitchell (63', 65'), Latham (74')
2 Conversions: Shepherd (63', 74')
1 Penalty: Huxley (2')

Canada

15	D. Van der Merwe (E. Fairhurst, 75')
14	J. Mensah-Coker
13	M. Pyke
12	D. Daypuck (N. Trenkel, 67')
11	J. Pritchard
10	A. Monro
9	M. Williams (cap.)
8	S. Stephen (M. Webb, 53')
7	D. Biddle
6	C. Yukes
5	M. James (M. Burak, 64')
4	L. Tait
3	J. Thiel
2	P. Riordan (A. Carpenter, 46')
1	R. Snow (D. Pletch, 53'-73')

2 Penalties: Pritchard (43', 54')

Match 36
SATURDAY 29 SEPTEMBER
POOL B

Fiji's elusive Vilimoni Delasau escapes the clutches of Alun Wyn Jones.

Fiji — Wales:
38–34

NANTES, Stade de la Beaujoire
Attendance: 37,080
Referee: Stuart Dickinson (AUS)

Fiji

15	K. Ratuvou
14	V. Delasau
13	S. Rabeni (N. Ligairi, 67')
12	S. Baï
11	I. Neivua (S. Bobo, 52')
10	N. Little (J. Daunivucu, 80')
9	M. Rauluni (cap.)
8	S. Koyamaibole
7	A. Qera (A. Ratuva, 74')
6	S. Naevo (N. Talei, 62')
5	I. Rawaqa
4	K. Leawere
3	J. Railomo (H. Qiodravu, 55')
2	S. Koto (V. Sauturaga, 77')
1	G. Dewes

4 Tries: Qera (16'), Delasau (19'), Leawere (25'), Dewes (77')
3 Conversions: Little (16', 25', 77')
4 Penalties: Little (21', 23', 53', 59')
1 Yellow Card: Qera (39')

Wales

15	G. Thomas (cap.)
14	M. Jones
13	T. Shanklin
12	J. Hook
11	S. Williams
10	S. Jones
9	D. Peel (M. Phillips, 58')
8	A. Popham (M. Owen, 66')
7	M. Williams
6	C. Charvis
5	I. Evans (I. Gough, 66')
4	A. W. Jones
3	C. Horsman (D. Jones, 66')
2	M. Rees (R. Thomas, 47')
1	G. Jenkins

5 Tries: Popham (34'), S. Williams (45'), G. Thomas (48'), M. Jones (51'), M. Williams (73')
3 Conversions: Hook (34'), S. Jones (45', 51')
1 Penalty: S. Jones (5')

Match 37
SATURDAY 29 SEPTEMBER
POOL C

The Scottish kicking sent Mike Blair and his team into the quarter-finals.

Scotland – Italy:
18–16

ST-ÉTIENNE, Stade Geoffroy-Guichard
Attendance : 34,701
Referee: Jonathan Kaplan (RSA)

Scotland

15	R. Lamont (H. Southwell, 25')
14	S. Lamont
13	S. Webster
12	R. Dewey (A. Henderson, 60')
11	C. Paterson
10	D. Parks
9	M. Blair (C. Cusiter, 73')
8	S. Taylor
7	A. Hogg (K. Brown, 70')
6	J. White (cap.)
5	J. Hamilton (S. MacLeod, 73')
4	N. Hines
3	E. Murray
2	R. Ford
1	G. Kerr (C. Smith, 65')

6 Penalties: Paterson (2', 5', 32', 35', 47', 52')
1 Yellow Card: Hines (54')

Italy

15	D. Bortolussi
14	K. Robertson
13	G. Canale
12	Mi. Bergamasco
11	A. Masi (E. Galon, 79')
10	R. Pez
9	A. Troncon (cap.)
8	S. Parisse
7	Ma. Bergamasco
6	J. Sole
5	C. Del Fava
4	A. Dellape
3	L. Castrogiovanni (A. Lo Cicero, 75')
2	C. Festuccia (F. Ongaro, 54')
1	S. Perugini (A. Lo Cicero, 49'-75')

1 Try: Troncon (12')
1 Conversions: Bortolussi (12')
3 Penalties: Bortolussi (16', 56', 62')

Match 38
SUNDAY 30 SEPTEMBER

POOL D

Christophe Dominici and the French team put on an attacking display.

France – Georgia:
64–7

MARSEILLE, Stade Vélodrome
Attendance: 57,000
Referee: Alan Lewis (IRE)

France

15	C. Poitrenaud (V. Clerc, 73')
14	A. Rougerie
13	D. Marty (D. Skrela, 58')
12	Y. Jauzion
11	C. Dominici
10	L. Beauxis
9	P. Mignoni (J.-B. Élissalde, 21')
8	J. Bonnaire
7	Y. Nyanga
6	S. Betsen (cap.) (R. Martin, 64')
5	J. Thion (F. Pelous, 53')
4	L. Nallet
3	J.-B. Poux (N. Mas, 58')
2	S. Bruno (D. Szarzewski, 58')
1	O. Milloud

9 Tries: Poitrenaud (6'), Nyanga (29'), Beauxis (36'), Dominici (45', 56'), Bruno (52'), Nallet (62'), Martin (66'), Bonnaire (79')
5 Conversions.: Beauxis (6', 29', 36', 52', 62')
3 Penalties: Beauxis (3', 17', 24')

Georgia

15	O. Barkalaia (O. Eloshvili, 54')
14	M. Urjukashvili
13	R. Gigauri
12	I. Giorgadze
11	B. Khamashuridze (G. Elizbarashvili, 54')
10	M. Kvirikashvili
9	I. Abuseridze (cap.) (B. Samkharadze, 30')
8	G. Chkhaidze
7	R. Urushadze
6	I. Maisuradze (Z. Maisuradze, 48')
5	Z. Mtchedlichvili
4	V. Didebulidze (L. Datunashvili, 40')
3	D. Zirakashvili
2	A. Giorgadze
1	M. Magrakvelidze (G. Shvelidze, 48')

1 Try: Z. Maisuradze (71')
1 Conversion: Kvirikashvili (71')
2 Yellow Cards: Magrakvelidze (28'), Gigauri (75')

Match 39
SUNDAY 30 SEPTEMBER

POOL D

Brian O'Driscoll's try for Ireland did not dampen the Argentinean spirit.

Argentina – Ireland:
30–15

PARIS, Parc des Princes
Attendance: 45,450
Referee: Paul Honiss (NZL)

Argentine

15	I. Corleto
14	L. Borges
13	M. Contepomi (H. Senillosa, 70')
12	F. Contepomi
11	H. Agulla
10	J. M. Hernández
9	A. Pichot (cap.)
8	G. Longo
7	J. M. Fernández Lobbe
6	L. Ostiglia (M. Durand, 62')
5	P. Albacete
4	I. Fernandez Lobbe (R. Alvarez-Kairelis, 54')
3	M. Scelzo (O. Hasan, 77')
2	M. Ledesma (A. Vernet Basualdo, 79')
1	R. Roncero

2 Tries: Borges (17'), Agulla (39')
1 Conversion: F. Contepomi (40')
3 Penalties: F. Contepomi (42', 62', 66')
3 Drop Goals: Hernández (21', 35', 79')

Ireland

15	G. Murphy
14	S. Horgan
13	B. O'Driscoll (cap.)
12	G. D'Arcy
11	D. Hickie (G. Duffy, 70')
10	R. O'Gara
9	E. Reddan (I. Boss, 66')
8	D. Leamy
7	D. Wallace (N. Best, 65')
6	S. Easterby
5	P. O'Connell
4	D. O'Callaghan (M. O'Kelly, 65')
3	J. Hayes
2	J. Flannery (R. Best, 65')
1	M. Horan

2 Tries: O'Driscoll (32'), Murphy (47')
1 Conversion: O'Gara (32')
1 Penalty : O'Gara (20')

Match 40
SUNDAY 30 SEPTEMBER

POOL A

A double for the prolific try-scorer Bryan Habana.

South Africa – USA:
64–15

MONTPELLIER, Stade de la Mosson
Attendance: 30,485
Referee: Tony Spreadbury (ENG)

South Africa

15	P. Montgomery (R. Pienaar, 67')
14	A. Ndungane
13	J. Fourie
12	F. Steyn (A. Pretorius, 67')
11	B. Habana (J.-P. Pietersen, 53')
10	B. James
9	F. Du Preez
8	S. Burger
7	J. Smith
6	W. Van Heerden (Ba. Botha, 55' then B. Skinstad, 71')
5	V. Matfield
4	A. Van den Berg
3	B.J. Botha (C.J. Van der Linde, 25')
2	J. Smit (cap.)
1	O. Du Randt (B. Du Plessis, 72')

9 Tries: Burger (9'), Steyn (27'), Habana (35', 41'), Van der Linde (48'), Du Preez (53'), Fourie (61', 73'), Smith (76')
8 Conversions: Montgomery (9', 27', 35', 48', 53', 61'), James (73', 76')
1 Penalty: Montgomery (16')

United States

15	C. Wyles (V. Malifa, 75')
14	T. Ngwenya
13	P. Eloff
12	V. Esikia
11	S. Sika (T. Palamo, 75')
10	M. Hercus (cap.)
9	C. Erskine (M. Petri, 75')
8	D. Payne
7	T. Clever (M. Aylor, 54')
6	L. Stanfill (H. Bloomfield, 75')
5	M. Mangan
4	A. Parker
3	C. Osentowski
2	O. Lentz (B. Burdette, 75')
1	M. McDonald (M. Moekiola, 49')

2 Tries: Ngwenya (39'), Wyles (51')
1 Conversion: Hercus (39')
1 Penalty: Hercus (19')
1 Yellow Card: Clever (23')

Match 41
SATURDAY 6 OCTOBER

QF1

Three Wallabies are not enough to stop England's Paul Sackey.

England – Australia:
12–10

MARSEILLE, Stade Vélodrome
Attendance: 60,000
Referee: Alain Rolland (IRE)

England

15	J. Robinson
14	P. Sackey
13	M. Tait
12	M. Catt (T. Flood, 64')
11	J. Lewsey
10	J. Wilkinson
9	A. Gomarsall (P. Richards, 23'–26')
8	L. Moody (J. Worsley, 66')
7	N. Easter (L. Dallaglio, 69')
6	M. Corry
5	B. Kay
4	S. Shaw
3	P. Vickery (cap.) (M. Stevens, 59')
2	M. Regan (G. Chuter, 52')
1	A. Sheridan

4 Penalties: Wilkinson (21', 25', 51', 60')

Australia

15	C. Latham
14	A. Ashley-Cooper (D. Mitchell, 64')
13	S. Mortlock (cap.)
12	M. Giteau
11	L. Tuqiri
10	B. Barnes
9	G. Gregan
8	W. Palu (S. Hoiles, 76')
7	G. Smith (P. Waugh, 66')
6	R. Elsom (H. McMeniman, 64')
5	D. Vickerman
4	N. Sharpe
3	G. Shepherdson (A. Baxter, 66')
2	S. Moore (A. Freier, 73')
1	M. Dunning

1 Try: Tuqiri (33')
1 Conversion: Mortlock (33')
1 Penalty: Mortlock (6')

149

Match 42
SATURDAY 6 OCTOBER
QF2

Sébastian Chabal and the Blues, the nemesis of the All Blacks.

France – New Zealand:
20–18

CARDIFF, Millennium Stadium
Attendance: 71,699
Referee: Wayne Barnes (ENG)

France

15	D. Traille
14	V. Clerc
13	D. Marty
12	Y. Jauzion
11	C. Heymans (C. Dominici, 70')
10	L. Beauxis (F. Michalak, 68')
9	J.-B. Élissalde
8	J. Bonnaire
7	T. Dusautoir
6	S. Betsen (I. Harinordoquy, 5')
5	J. Thion
4	F. Pelous (S. Chabal, 52')
3	P. De Villiers
2	R. Ibañez (cap.) (D. Szarzewski, 52')
1	O. Milloud (J.-B. Poux, 41')

2 Tries: Dusautoir (54'), Jauzion (69')
2 Conversions: Beauxis (54'), Élissalde (69')
2 Penalties: Beauxis (40', 46')

New Zealand

15	L. MacDonald
14	J. Rokocoko
13	M. Muliaina
12	L. McAlister
11	S. Sivivatu
10	D. Carter (N. Evans, 56', then I. Toeava, 71')
9	B. Kelleher (B. Leonard, 56')
8	R. So'oialo
7	R. McCaw (cap.)
6	J. Collins (C. Masoe, 64')
5	A. Williams
4	K. Robinson (C. Jack, 50')
3	C. Hayman
2	A. Oliver (A. Hore, 56')
1	T. Woodcock

2 Tries: McAlister (17'), So'oialo (63')
1 Conversion: Carter (17')
2 Penalties: Carter (13', 30')
1 Yellow Card: McAlister (46')

Match 43
SUNDAY 7 OCTOBER
QF3

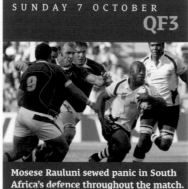

Mosese Rauluni sewed panic in South Africa's defence throughout the match.

South Africa – Fiji:
37–20

MARSEILLE, Stade Vélodrome
Attendance: 55,943
Referee: Alan Lewis (IRL)

South Africa

15	P. Montgomery
14	J.-P. Pietersen
13	J. Fourie
12	F. Steyn
11	B. Habana
10	B. James
9	F. Du Preez
8	D. Rossouw (W. Van Heerden, 50')
7	J. Smith
6	S. Burger
5	V. Matfield
4	Ba. Botha (J. Muller, 75')
3	J. Du Plessis
2	J. Smit (cap.)
1	O. Du Randt (G. Steenkamp, 53')

5 Tries: Fourie (14'), Smit (35'), Pietersen (50'), Smith (69'), James (80')
3 Conversions: Montgomery (50', 69', 80')
2 Penalties: Steyn (10'), Montgomery (63')

Fiji

15	N. Ligairi
14	V. Delasau
13	K. Ratuvou (G. Lovobalavu, 64')
12	S. Rabeni
11	S. Bobo
10	S. Baï
9	M. Rauluni (cap.)
8	A. Qera (A. Ratuva, 71')
7	S. Koyamaibole
6	S. Naevo
5	I. Rawaqa
4	K. Leawere (W. Lewaravu, 73')
3	H. Qiodravu (J. Railomo, 55')
2	S. Koto (B. Gadolo, 71')
1	G. Dewes

2 Tries: Delasau (57'), Bobo (59')
2 Conversions: Baï (57', 59')
2 Penalties: Baï (25', 44')
1 Yellow Card: Rabeni (51')

Match 44
SUNDAY 7 OCTOBER
QF4

A historic triumph for the two Juan Martíns, Hernández and Fernández Lobbe.

Argentina – Scotland:
19–13

SAINT-DENIS, Stade de France
Attendance: 79,866
Referee: Joël Jutge (FRA)

Argentina

15	I. Corleto
14	L. Borges
13	M. Contepomi (H. Senillosa, 67')
12	F. Contepomi
11	H. Agulla
10	J. M. Hernández
9	A. Pichot (cap.)
8	G. Longo
7	J. M. Fernández Lobbe
6	L. Ostiglia (J. Leguizamon, 55')
5	P. Albacete
4	I. Fernández Lobbe (R. Alvarez-Kairelis, 51')
3	M. Scelzo (O. Hasan, 57')
2	M. Ledesma
1	R. Roncero

1 Try: Longo (33')
1 Conversion: F. Contepomi (33')
3 Penalties: F. Contepomi (22', 28', 42')
1 Drop Goal: Hernández (54')

Scotland

15	R. Lamont (H. Southwell, 68')
14	S. Lamont
13	S. Webster
12	R. Dewey (A. Henderson, 41')
11	C. Paterson
10	D. Parks
9	M. Blair (C. Cusiter, 57')
8	A. Hogg (K. Brown, 57')
7	S. Taylor
6	J. White (cap.)
5	J. Hamilton (S. MacLeod, 57')
4	N. Hines
3	E. Murray
2	R. Ford (S. Lawson, 68')
1	G. Kerr (C. Smith, 57')

1 Try: Cusiter (63')
1 Conversion: Paterson (63')
2 Penalties: Parks (15'), Paterson (37')

Match 45
SATURDAY 13 OCTOBER
SF1

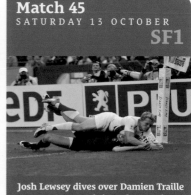

Josh Lewsey dives over Damien Traille to score 80 seconds into the match.

England – France:
14–9

SAINT-DENIS, Stade de France
Attendance: 80,283
Referee: Jonathan Kaplan (RSA)

England

15	J. Robinson
14	P. Sackey
13	M. Tait
12	M. Catt (T. Flood, 69')
11	J. Lewsey (D. Hipkiss, 47')
10	J. Wilkinson
9	A. Gomarsall (P. Richards, 71')
8	N. Easter (L. Dallaglio, 69')
7	L. Moody (J. Worsley, 54')
6	M. Corry
5	B. Kay
4	S. Shaw
3	P. Vickery (cap.) (M. Stevens, 56')
2	M. Regan
1	A. Sheridan (G. Chuter, 66')

1 Try: Lewsey (2')
2 Penalties: Wilkinson (46', 74')
1 Drop-Goal: Wilkinson (78')

France

15	D. Traille
14	V. Clerc
13	D. Marty
12	Y. Jauzion
11	C. Heymans (C. Dominici, 60')
10	L. Beauxis (F. Michalak, 51')
9	J.-B. Élissalde
8	J. Bonnaire
7	T. Dusautoir
6	S. Betsen (I. Harinordoquy, 67')
5	J. Thion
4	F. Pelous (S. Chabal, 25')
3	P. De Villiers (J.-B. Poux, 66')
2	R. Ibañez (cap.) (D. Szarzewski, 51')
1	O. Milloud

3 Penalties: Beauxis (7', 17', 43')

150

Match 46
SUNDAY 14 OCTOBER

SF2

Fourie Du Preez shatters the Argentinean defence.

South Africa – Argentina:
37–13

SAINT-DENIS, Stade de France
Attendance: 80,000
Referee: Steve Walsh (NZL)

South Africa

15	P. Montgomery
14	J.-P. Pietersen (R. Pienaar, 76')
13	J. Fourie
12	F. Steyn (W. Olivier, 76')
11	B. Habana
10	B. James (A. Pretorius, 76')
9	F. Du Preez
8	D. Rossouw (B. Skinstad, 75')
7	J. Smith
6	S. Burger
5	V. Matfield
4	Ba. Botha (J. Muller, 22'–28', then permanently, 76')
3	CJ Van der Linde
2	J. Smit (cap.) (B. Du Plessis, 76')
1	O. Du Randt

4 Tries: Du Preez (7'), Habana (32', 75'), Rossouw (40')
4 Conversions: Montgomery (7', 32', 40', 75')
3 Penalties: Montgomery (16', 70', 74')
1 Yellow Card: Smith (78')

Argentina

15	I. Corleto
14	L. Borges
13	M. Contepomi (G. Tiesi, 64')
12	F. Contepomi
11	H. Agulla
10	J. M. Hernández
9	A. Pichot (cap.)
8	G. Longo
7	J. M. Fernández Lobbe
6	L. Ostiglia (J. Leguizamon, 64')
5	P. Albacete
4	I. Fernández Lobbe (R. Alvarez-Kairelis, 53')
3	M. Scelzo (O. Hasan, 34')
2	M. Ledesma
1	R. Roncero

1 Try: M. Contepomi (45')
1 Conversion: F. Contepomi (45')
1 Penalty: F. Contepomi (14', 28')
1 Yellow Card: F. Contepomi (79')

Match 47
FRIDAY 19 OCTOBER

3rd PLACE

The sky falls in on Clément Poitrenaud and the Blues.

Argentina – France:
34–10

PARIS, Parc des Princes
Attendance: 45,958
Referee: Paul Honiss (NZL)

Argentina

15	I. Corleto (F. Todeschini, 74')
14	F. Martin Aramburu
13	M. Contepomi (H. Senillosa, 60')
12	F. Contepomi
11	H. Agulla
10	J. M. Hernandez
9	A. Pichot (cap.) (N. Fernandez Miranda, 68')
8	G. Longo
7	I. Fernandez Lobbe
6	M. Durand (J. Leguizamon, 60')
5	P. Albacete
4	R. Alvarez-Kairelis (E. Lozada, 71')
3	O. Hasan (M. Ayerza, 71')
2	A. Vernet Basualdo
1	R. Roncero

5 Tries: F. Contepomi (28', 77'), Hasan (31'), Martin Aramburu (54'), Corleto (65')
3 Conversions: F. Contepomi (28', 31', 77')
1 Penalty: F. Contepomi (20e)
2 Yellow Cards: R. Alvarez-Kairelis (40'), J. Leguizamon (63')

France

15	C. Poitrenaud
14	A. Rougerie (V. Clerc, 61')
13	D. Skrela
12	D. Marty (L. Beauxis, 63')
11	C. Dominici
10	F. Michalak
9	J.-B. Élissalde (P. Mignoni, 55')
8	I. Harinordoquy
7	T. Dusautoir (R. Martin, 51')
6	Y. Nyanga
5	J. Thion (S. Chabal, 61')
4	L. Nallet
3	N. Mas
2	R. Ibañez (cap.) (S. Bruno, 41')
1	J.-B. Poux

1 Try: Poitrenaud (67')
1 Conversion: Beauxis (67')
1 Penalty: Élissalde (18')
1 Yellow Card: Ibañez (40')

Match 48
SATURDAY 20 OCTOBER

FINAL

The French president Nicolas Sarkozy congratulates winning captain John Smit.

South Africa – England:
15–6

SAINT-DENIS, Stade de France
Attendance: 80,430
Referee: Alain Rolland (IRE)

South Africa

15	P. Montgomery
14	J.-P. Pietersen
13	J. Fourie
12	F. Steyn
11	B. Habana
10	B. James
9	F. Du Preez
8	D. Rossouw (W. Van Heerden, 73')
7	J. Smith
6	S. Burger
5	V. Matfield
4	Ba. Botha
3	CJ Van der Linde
2	J. Smit (cap.) (B. Du Plessis, 72'–75')
1	O. Du Randt

5 Penalties: Montgomery (7', 15', 39', 50'), Steyn (61')

England

15	J. Robinson (D. Hipkiss, 47')
14	P. Sackey
13	M. Tait
12	M. Catt (T. Flood, 51')
11	M. Cueto
10	J. Wilkinson
9	A. Gomarsall
8	L. Moody (J. Worsley, 63', then P. Richards, 79')
7	N. Easter (L. Dallaglio, 65')
6	M. Corry
5	B. Kay
4	S. Shaw
3	P. Vickery (M. Stevens, 41')
2	M. Regan (G. Chuter, 63')
1	A. Sheridan

2 Penalties: Wilkinson (11', 43')

Players

TRIES

Leading try scorers, RWC 2007

8 Bryan HABANA
(RSA)

7 Drew MITCHELL
(AUS)

6 Doug HOWLETT
(NZL)

Shane WILLIAMS
(WAL)

5 Vincent CLERC
(FRA)

Joe ROKOCOKO
(NZL)

Chris LATHAM
(AUS)

In a single RWC 2007 match

4 Bryan HABANA
(RSA, v. Samoa)

3 Doug HOWLETT
(NZL, v. Italy)

Rocky ELSOM
(AUS, v. Japan)

Vincent CLERC
(FRA, v. Namibia)

Allister HOGG
(SCO, v. Romania)

Drew MITCHELL
(AUS, v. Fiji)

Joe ROKOCOKO
(NZL, v. Romania)

All-time in the RWC

15 Jonah LOMU
(NZL)

13 Doug HOWLETT
(NZL)

11 Rory UNDERWOOD
(ENG)

Joe ROKOCOKO
(NZL)

Chris LATHAM (AUS)

In a single RWC match all-time

6 Marc ELLIS
(NZL, v. Japan, 1995)

POINTS

Leading points scorers, RWC 2007

105 Percy MONTGOMERY
(RSA)

91 Felipe CONTEPOMI
(ARG)

67 Jonny WILKINSON
(ENG)

50 Nick EVANS
(NZL)

47 J.-Baptiste ÉLISSALDE
(FRA)

46 Chris PATERSON
(SCO)

44 Pierre HOLA
(TON)

43 Lionel BEAUXIS
(FRA)

42 Nicky LITTLE
(FIJ)

In a single RWC 2007 match

33 Nick EVANS
(NZL, v. Portugal)

29 Percy MONTGOMERY
(RSA, v. Samoa)

27 J.-Baptiste ÉLISSALDE
(FRA, v. Namibia)

Matt GITEAU
(AUS, v. Fiji)

24 Jonny WILKINSON
(ENG, v. Samoa)

Lionel BEAUXIS
(FRA, v. Georgia)

All-time in the RWC

249 Jonny WILKINSON
(ENG)

227 Gavin HASTINGS
(SCO)

195 Michael LYNAGH
(AUS)

In a single RWC match all-time

45 Simon CULHANE
(NZL, v. Japan, 1995)

PENALTIES

Leading penalty kickers, RWC 2007

18 Felipe CONTEPOMI
(ARG)

17 Percy MONTGOMERY
(RSA)

14 Jonny WILKINSON
(ENG)

10 Pierre HOLA
(TON)

8 David BORTOLUSSI
(ITA)

Nicky LITTLE
(FIJ)

Lionel BEAUXIS
(FRA)

In a single RWC 2007 match

6 Chris PATERSON
(SCO, v. Italy)

5 Loki CHRICHTON
(SAM, v. England)

Gavin WILLIAMS
(SAM, v. Tonga)

J.-Baptiste ÉLISSALDE
(FRA, v. Ireland)

All-time in the RWC

53 Jonny WILKINSON
(ENG)

36 Gavin HASTINGS
(SCO)

35 Gonzalo QUESADA
(ARG)

33 Andrew MEHRTENS
(NZL)

Michael LYNAGH (AUS)

In a single RWC match all-time

8 Matt BURKE
(AUS, v. South Africa, 1999)

Gonzalo QUESADA
(ARG, v. Samoa, 1999)

Thierry LACROIX
(FRA, v. Ireland, 1995)

Gavin HASTINGS
(SCO, v. Tonga, 1995)

CONVERSIONS

Leading conversion kickers, RWC 2007

22	Percy MONTGOMERY	(RSA)
20	Nick EVANS	(NZL)
12	J.-Baptiste ÉLISSALDE	(FRA)
11	Felipe CONTEPOMI	(ARG)
	Stephen JONES	(WAL)

In a single RWC 2007 match

14	Nick EVANS	(NZL, v. Portugal)
11	J.-Baptiste ÉLISSALDE	(FRA, v. Namibia)
7	Dan CARTER	(NZL, v. Italy)
	Stirling MORTLOCK	(AUS, v. Japan)

All-time in the RWC

39	Gavin HASTINGS	(SCO)
37	Grant FOX	(NZL)
36	Michael LYNAGH	(AUS)
29	Dan CARTER	(NZL)
27	Paul GRAYSON	(ENG)

In a single RWC match all-time

20	Simon CULHANE	(NZL, v. Japan, 1995)
16	Mat ROGERS	(AUS, v. Namibia, 2003)
14	Nick EVANS	(NZL, v. Portugal, 2007.)

DROP GOALS

Leading drop-goal kickers, RWC 2007

5	Jonny WILKINSON	(ENG)
4	Juan M. HERNANDEZ	(ARG)
3	Berrick BARNES	(AUS)
1	Ronan O'GARA	(IRE)
	Émile WESSELS	(NAM)
	Gonçalo MALHEIRO	(POR)

In a single RWC 2007 match

3	Juan M. HERNANDEZ	(ARG, v. Ireland)
2	Jonny WILKINSON	(ENG, v. Samoa)
	Jonny WILKINSON	(ENG, v. Tonga)

All-time in the RWC

13	Jonny WILKINSON	(ENG)
6	Jannie DE BEER	(RSA)
5	Rob ANDREW	(ENG)
	Gareth REES	(CAN)

In a single RWC match all-time

5	Jannie DE BEER	RSA, v. England, 1999
3	Juan M. HERNANDEZ	(ARG, v. Ireland, 2007)
	Jonny WILKINSON	(ENG, v. France, 2003)

SUCCESS RATE

Highest kicking percentage in RWC 2007 (minimum 3 attempts)

100 %	Chris PATERSON	(SCO, 17 out of 17)
90.9 %	Nick EVANS	(NZL, 20 out of 22)
	Loki CHRICHTON	(SAM, 10 out of 11)
85.7 %	Dan PARKS	(SCO, 6 out of 7)
83.3 %	Ollie BARKLEY	(ENG, 5 out of 6)

APPEARANCES IN THE RWC

22	Jason LEONARD	(ENG)
20	George GREGAN	(AUS)
19	Mike CATT	(ENG)
18	Brian LIMA	(SAM)
	Raphaël IBAÑEZ	(FRA)
	Martin JOHNSON	(ENG)
17	Lawrence DALLAGLIO	(ENG)
	Sean FITZPATRICK	(NZL)
16	Os DU RANDT	(RSA)
	Phil VICKERY	(ENG)
	Fabien PELOUS	(FRA)

ABBREVIATIONS

RWC: Rugby World Cup, ARG: Argentina, AUS: Australia, CAN: Canada, ENG: England, FIJ: Fiji, FRA: France, GEO: Georgia, IRE: Ireland, ITA: Italy, JAP: Japan, NAM: Namibia, NZL: New Zealand, POR: Portugal, ROM: Romania, RSA: South Africa, SAM: Samoa, SCO: Scotland, TON: Tonga, USA: United States, WAL: Wales

Teams

TRIES

Leading try scorers, RWC 2007

48 NEW ZEALAND
33 South Africa
31 Australia
27 France
23 Argentina
Wales
16 Fiji
15 Scotland

Highest average number of tries scored per match, RWC 2007

9.6 NEW ZEALAND
6.2 Australia
5.8 Wales
4.7 South Africa
3.9 France

Most tries scored in a single match in the RWC 2007

16 NEW ZEALAND
(v. Portugal)
13 France
(v. Namibia)
Australia
(v. Japan)
New Zealand
(v. Romania)
11 Wales
(v. Japan)
New Zealand
(v. Italy)

Most tries scored in a single match all-time in the RWC

22 AUSTRALIA
(v. Namibia, 2003)
21 New Zealand
(v. Japan, 1995)
17 England
(v. Uruguay, 2003)

POINTS SCORED

Leading points scorers, RWC 2007

327 NEW ZEALAND
278 South Africa
227 France
225 Australia
209 Argentina
168 Wales
140 England
134 Fiji

Highest average of points per game scored, RWC 2007

65.4 NEW ZEALAND
45 Australia
42 Wales
39.7 South Africa
32.4 France

Most points scored in a single match in the RWC 2007

108 NEW ZEALAND
(v. Portugal)
91 Australia
(v. Japan)
87 France
(v. Namibia)
85 New Zealand
(v. Romania)

Most points scored in a single match all-time in the RWC

145 NEW ZEALAND
(v. Japan, 1995)
142 Australia
(v. Namibia, 2003)
111 England
(v. Uruguay, 2003)
108 New Zealand
(v. Portugal, 2007)
101 England
(v. Tonga, 1999)

POINTS CONCEDED

Fewest points conceded, RWC 2007

53 AUSTRALIA
55 New Zealand
75 Scotland
82 Ireland
86 South Africa
93 Argentina

Lowest average of points per game conceded, RWC 2007

10.6 AUSTRALIA
11 New Zealand
12.3 South Africa
13.3 Argentina
15 France

Fewest points conceded in a single match in the RWC 2007

0 Scotland
(v. Romania)
New Zealand
(v. Scotland)
South Africa
(v. England, Pool match)
Georgia
(v. Namibia)

CARDS

Red cards shown, RWC 2007

1 NAMIBIA, TONGA

Most yellow cards shown, RWC 2007

4 UNITED STATES
3 Fiji, Tonga, South Africa, Argentina, Italy

SCORES

Biggest winning margins, RWC 2007

95 pts New Zealand v. Portugal (108–13)

88 pts Australia v. Japan (91–3)

77 pts France v. Namibia (87–10)

New Zealand v. Romania (85–8)

62 pts New Zealand v. Italy (76–14)

60 pts Argentina v. Namibia (63–3)

57 pts France v. Georgia (64–7)

54 pts Wales v. Japan (72–18)

52 pts South Africa v. Samoa (59–7)

49 pts South Africa v. United States (64–15)

Biggest winning margins all-time in the RWC

142 pts Australia v. Namibia (142–0, 2003)

128 pts New Zealand v. Japan (145–17, 1995)

98 pts New Zealand v. Italy (101–3, 1999)

England v. Uruguay (111–13, 2003)

95 pts New Zealand v. Portugal (108–13, 2007)

PENALTIES

Highest number of penalties kicked, RWC 2007

21 SOUTH AFRICA

18 Argentina

France

17 England

Most penalties kicked in a single game in the RWC 2007

6 SCOTLAND (v. Italy)

5 South Africa (v. England, Pool match and final)

Samoa (v. Tonga and v. England)

France (v. Ireland)

CONVERSIONS

Highest number of conversions kicked, RWC 2007

36 NEW ZEALAND

25 South Africa

20 Australia

Highest number of conversions kicked in a single match in the RWC 2007

14 NEW ZEALAND (v. Portugal)

11 FRANCE (v. Namibia)

10 Australia (v. Japan)

New Zealand (v. Romania)

DROP GOALS

Highest number of drop goals kicked, RWC 2007

5 ENGLAND

4 Argentina

3 Australia

Highest number of drop goals kicked in a single match in the RWC 2007

3 ARGENTINA (v. Ireland)

2 England (v. Samoa and v. Tonga)

ABBREVIATIONS

RWC: Rugby World Cup

Pts: points

P: Number of matches played

W: Number of wins

D: Number of draws

L: Number of defeats

PF: points for

PA: points against

B: bonus points (1 attacking bonus point for scoring four tries or more in a match; 1 defensive bonus point for a defeat by seven points or fewer)

POOL TABLES

Pool A

	Pts	P	W	D	L	PF	PA	B
1. SOUTH AFRICA	19	4	4	0	0	189	47	3
2. ENGLAND	14	4	3	0	1	108	88	2
3. Tonga	9	4	2	0	2	89	96	1
4. Samoa	5	4	1	0	3	69	143	1
5. United States	1	4	0	0	4	61	142	1

Pool B

	Pts	P	W	D	L	PF	PA	B
1. AUSTRALIA	20	4	4	0	0	215	41	4
2. FIJI	15	4	3	0	1	114	136	3
3. Wales	12	4	2	0	2	168	105	4
4. Japan	3	4	0	1	3	64	210	1
5. Canada	2	4	0	1	3	51	120	0

Pool C

	Pts	P	W	D	L	PF	PA	B
1. NEW ZEALAND	20	4	4	0	0	309	35	4
2. SCOTLAND	14	4	3	0	1	116	66	2
3. Italy	9	4	2	0	2	85	117	1
4. Romania	5	4	1	0	3	40	161	1
5. Portugal	1	4	0	0	4	38	209	1

Pool D

	Pts	P	W	D	L	PF	PA	B
1. ARGENTINA	18	4	4	0	0	143	33	2
2. FRANCE	15	4	3	0	1	188	37	3
3. Ireland	9	4	2	0	2	64	82	1
4. Georgia	5	4	1	0	3	50	111	1
5. Namibia	0	4	0	0	4	30	212	0

PICTURE CREDITS

For seven weeks, the lenses of the world's photographers were exclusively focused on the best rugby players on the planet.